PROFILES
OF GREAT
AFRICAN
AMERICANS

CONTRIBUTING WRITERS

DAVID SMALLWOOD
STAN WEST
ALLISON KEYES

CONSULTANTS

CHARLES R. BRANHAM, Ph.D.
JEAN CURRIE CHURCH
JOYCE ANN JOYCE, Ph.D.

PUBLICATIONS INTERNATIONAL, LTD.

David Smallwood is associate editor of *N'Digo,* a bimonthly Chicago magazine for African Americans. He is the former entertainment editor for *Jet* magazine, and was a journalism writing instructor at Columbia College. He is a freelance writer for both print and television, and is a speechwriter.

Stan West is a writer, former associate editor of the *Chicago Daily Defender,* and producer and talk show host on Chicago's WNUA-FM. He is the author of *Prism: An African-American Reporter's Multi-Cultural View of the New South Africa* and coauthor of *Why L.A. Happened: Implications of the '92 Rebellion.* He was nominated for an Emmy for his 90-minute WTTW-TV show *Combating Racism: Where To Begin?*

Allison Keyes is a line producer for New York 1 News, the Time-Warner 24-hour cable news station. She is a former newswriter and producer for ABC affiliate WLS-TV Chicago, reporter and columnist for *N'Digo* magazine, and political editor and anchor for National Public Radio's WBEZ-FM. She is a member of the National Association of Black Journalists and the former vice president of the Chicago Association of Black Journalists.

Charles R. Branham, Ph.D., is senior historian for the DuSable Museum of African American History in Chicago, and adjunct professor of Minority Studies at Indiana University Northwest. He was the writer and coproducer of *The Black Experience,* a series of 60 half-hour programs for Chicago's WTTW-TV. He is the author of *The Transformation of Black Political Leadership* and coauthor of *Black Chicago Accommodationist Politics Before the Great Migration.*

Jean Currie Church is the chief librarian for the Moorland-Spingarn Research Center, Howard University, a major repository of materials for the study of Black history and culture. She is a member of the American Library Association, the Black Caucus of the ALA, and the Academy of Certified Archivists.

Joyce Ann Joyce, Ph.D., is professor of English and associate director of the Gwendolyn Brooks Center at Chicago State University. She is the author of *Warriors, Conjurers, and Priests: Defining African-Centered Literary Criticism* and *Native Son: Richard Wright's Art of Tragedy.* She has coauthored several books, including *Langston Hughes: The Man, His Art, and His Influence.*

Editorial Assistant: Rosa L. Anthony

Special thanks to Donna Wells and Joseph Hill, Moorland-Spingarn Research Center, Howard University; and Jim Huffman, Schomburg Center for Research in Black Culture, Photographs and Prints Division, New York Public Library.

Right: *Edward "Duke" Ellington*

CONTENTS

C O N T E N T S

INTRODUCTION

T he African-American historical experience was forged in the crucible of struggle but it is more, much more, than merely the recorded history of that struggle. It is also the story of the transcendence and triumph of the human spirit, of remarkable men and women who challenged myths and misconceptions, hurdled barriers, blazed trails, invented, created, transformed, and reinvigorated our common culture and, in the process, refashioned our common American heritage. These extraordinary weavers of dreams and rewriters of record books are monuments to the pride and per-

sistence that has always permeated the African-American past and these men and women are but a small sample of the rich reservoir of ambition and energy that marks the diverse and still unfolding story of the African-American past.

Here are their stories: an unlettered slave who read her poetry to our first President; and a brilliant man of letters, one of the most catholic thinkers of the 20th century, who forsook the cloistered halls of academe to pursue a lifelong struggle for human rights. A boy, once traded for a horse, who would discover hundreds of uses for the peanut and sweet potato, and an apostle of nonviolence cut down by an assassin's bullet.

There is an irony here: "Moses" was a woman who led 300 slaves "out of the House of Bondage"; a brash young army officer who challenged racial segregation in the army would later demonstrate remarkable patience and forbearance in the face of catcalls and death threats as he shattered the color line of professional sports; a great composer would die unheralded and unknown, a half century later his music would provide the score for an Academy-Award-

Above: *Louis Armstrong brought jazz to the masses. He invented scat singing and the stop-time solo break. He also perfected "swing" jazz, where the notes are placed a fraction before or behind the beat.* Right: *Jackie Robinson forever changed the face of baseball by breaking the color line in 1946. He rebuked racism with superb talent and tolerance, and was the first African American elected to the Baseball Hall of Fame in 1962.*

winning movie and revive public appreciation of a forgotten musical genre.

Here Sojourner Truth asks plaintively "Aren't I a Woman?" Marcus Garvey commands "Up you Mighty Race! You can accomplish what you will!" Here Du-Sable explores, Ellington composes, and Michael Jordan soars high above the rim. Here Malcolm X undergoes a spiritual conversion in a dank prison cell, Ralph Bunche brokers peace in the Middle East, and Paul Robeson sacrifices a career for the cause of social justice. They are all here, the famous and the little known, the men and women whose lives have touched our lives, subtly, sometimes imperceptibly reshaping our world.

Of course, no selection of the "Greatest" is without controversy. It was not an easy task to select the names and, unquestionably, the debate will continue over their relative merits and notables who just missed making the list. Any list is at best an approximation, a starting point for discussion and debate.

But these profiles represent a beginning point, a serious attempt to briefly summarize the lives and contributions of African Americans in all of the rich and varied aspects of the American experience. If we stand taller and see farther, it is because we stand on the shoulders of these titans of the African-American past. We are indebted to them, their courage, their sacrifice; we are inspired by their example, and emboldened to create a future worthy of their legacy.

Charles Branham, Senior Historian
DuSable Museum of African American History

Left: George Washington Carver revolutionized farming in the South. He taught farmers to grown peanuts and sweet potatoes, rather than cotton, which robs soil of nutrients. Below: General Colin Powell was the first African American to serve as chairman of the Joint Chiefs of Staff. He also considered running for the presidency in 1996, but decided against it. Polls listed him as a very strong candidate.

I t was a record that most baseball fans thought would never be broken—Babe Ruth's 714 career home runs. But on April 8, 1974, in front of 53,775 fans in Fulton County Stadium, 40-year-old Henry Louis "Hammerin' Hank" Aaron blasted a fastball from pitcher Al Downing 385 feet to surpass Ruth's formidable achievement. Aaron went on to set the new record for home runs at 755 before he retired.

Aaron is arguably the most prolific baseball player of all time. In addition to holding the home run record, he has the most runs batted in with 2,297, is second in runs scored with 2,174, and third in hits with 3,771.

During his career, Aaron appeared in 24 All-Star Games. He's the only National League player to hit 40 or more homers in eight seasons and was the first player to collect 500 home runs and 3,000 hits. No slouch defensively, Aaron won Gold Gloves as the top right fielder from 1958 to 1960. As soon as he was eligible, in 1982, Aaron was voted into the Baseball Hall of Fame—quite an accomplishment for a kid who originally didn't know how to bat correctly.

Aaron was born on February 5, 1934, in segregated Mobile, Alabama, where his high school didn't have a baseball team. In honing his skills playing sandlot ball, Aaron originally batted with the wrong hand on top, but he had exceptionally quick wrists.

Nonetheless, he was impressive enough that the Indianapolis Clowns of the Negro leagues scouted him and offered the skinny, 17-year-old a $200-a-month contract in 1951. But his Negro league career would not last long. When Jackie Robinson joined the Brooklyn Dodgers in 1947 (he signed with the organization in 1945), breaking baseball's racial barrier, it was the beginning of the end of the Negro leagues. By 1952, the financially strapped Clowns sold Aaron's contract to the Milwaukee (now Atlanta) Braves.

In his first year in the minors, Aaron batted .336 and was named the Rookie of the Year. The next year, after moving up a level, he was named the league's Most Valuable Player (MVP).

In 1954, Aaron was called to the majors after the Braves' second

HANK AARON HIT HIS 649TH HOME RUN ON JUNE 10, 1972, TO PASS SECOND-PLACE WILLIE MAYS IN PURSUIT OF BABE RUTH'S CAREER MARK OF 714 DINGERS. DESPITE BEING HEAPED WITH RACIAL ABUSE, DEROGATORY LETTERS, AND DEATH THREATS, AARON KEPT HITTING HOME RUNS TO FINALLY BREAK RUTH'S RECORD ON APRIL 8, 1974.

baseman broke his ankle. In his first game, Aaron had three hits, including a mammoth home run. In 1955, he had an All-Star year statistically. In 1956, he led the National League in hitting with a .328 average and was considered one of the best players in the game.

Then, in 1957, he hit the home run that helped the Braves win the pennant, and hit three more home runs to help them capture the World Series. Aaron was also named league MVP that year, but 1957 was the only time he would win that award or a World Series championship.

Aaron retired after a 23-year major-league career, rewriting baseball's batting record books along the way. He holds more major-league batting records than any other player in history. He currently serves as senior vice president of the Atlanta Braves. He also sits on the National Board of the NAACP and the Sterling Committee of Morehouse College.

Left: *Aaron poses after being named the National League's Most Valuable Player in 1957. He edged out Stan Musial and teammate Red Schoendienst for the honor. He was also the home run and runs-batted-in king of the majors that season.* Right: *Aaron waits for his next chance at another home run.*

9

ROBERT S. ABBOTT

ROBERT S. ABBOTT

FOUNDED THE CHICAGO DEFENDER IN 1905. IT WOULD LATER BECOME THE MOST SUCCESSFUL, INFLUENTIAL, AND WIDELY CIRCULATED BLACK WEEKLY NEWSPAPER IN THE COUNTRY. ABBOTT STARTED THE PAPER WITH JUST 25 CENTS AND NO STAFF, BUT THE PAPER'S SUCCESS MADE HIM ONE OF CHICAGO'S FIRST BLACK MILLIONAIRES.

A legendary figure in the annals of American journalism, Robert Sengstacke Abbott founded the *Chicago Defender* in 1905. In its heyday, it was the most successful and influential Black newspaper in the country.

Abbott was born on November 24, 1870, to former slaves in St. Simon's Island, Georgia. But it was his stepfather, John Sengstacke, who aroused young Robert's passion to secure equal rights for African Americans. Abbott was so impressed with his stepfather that he later took Sengstacke as his middle name.

Abbott earned his law degree in 1898 from Chicago Kent College of Law and, for a few years, practiced in Gary, Indiana, and Topeka, Kansas. But he returned to Chicago with the dream of publishing what he called "The World's Greatest Weekly, the *Chicago Defender.*"

And though Abbott reportedly had only a total of 25 cents to undertake this great endeavor, he was not deterred. Financial support and articles written by friends kept him going—Abbott was a one-man gang. Working out of his small apartment, he peddled the *Defender* from door to door, and through barber shops, churches, bars, and poolrooms in Chicago's African-American community.

Though the city had a number of Black papers at the time, none matched the strong political and social stance Abbott had the *Defender* take. From the beginning, he intended the paper to be an important voice against racial oppression and injustice. That voice spurred a circulation growth that reached 230,000 only ten years after the paper started.

The *Defender* was distributed throughout the South by Pullman porters on the railway cars. So intense were Abbott's angry articles against lynching and oppression in the South that many historians credit him with being a primary cause of the great migration of Blacks from the South to the North during the 1920s and 1930s.

Abbott wanted the paper to speak for and provide advice to the Black community. As such, the *Defender* voiced the concerns and outrage Blacks felt—these opinions would never have seen print elsewhere.

The bloody Chicago Race Riot of July 1919 started when a group of Whites stoned

and drowned a young Black man who swam beyond an imaginary point in Lake Michigan that Blacks were not allowed to cross. There was much loss of life. Two years earlier, the *Defender* had pointed out that the pent-up anger of Blacks over jobs, housing, and politics would eventually lead to just such an explosive situation. The *Defender* gave exhaustive coverage to the five days of rioting. Afterward, Abbott was named a member of the Chicago Commission on Race Relations, which in 1922 published the frequently cited report "The Negro in Chicago." This report examined the causes of the 1919 riots and the great migration of Blacks to Chicago.

One of Abbott's important legacies was started in 1929, when he created the Bud Billiken "Back-to-School" Parade to promote education among Black children.

Abbott died of Bright's disease on February 29, 1940. At the time, the *Chicago Defender* was the most widely circulated Black weekly in the country.

Facing page: *Following in the tradition of legendary Black newspapers such as* Freedom's Journal, The North Star, The Guardian, New York Age, *and the* Pittsburgh Courier, *Robert Abbott ramrodded the* Chicago Defender *into becoming the most influential and widely circulated Black weekly newspaper in the country.* Left: *Abbott had a soft spot for children and in 1929 created the Bud Billiken "Back-to-School" parade, now one of the largest Black parades in the country.*

The colorful phrase "Float like a butterfly, sting like a bee," created by his cornerman Drew Bundini Brown, perfectly sums up the boxing style of Muhammad Ali, the self-proclaimed and widely acknowledged "greatest fighter of all time!"

He was the first man to win the heavyweight championship three times. Ali's astonishing speed, punishing punching power, brilliant footwork, awesome defensive skills, and lethal left jab contributed to his boxing legend. To watch him was to see a dancing Ali, circling, carving up an opponent with a jab too fast for his opponent to react to, while inviting punches that he gracefully slipped.

MUHAMMAD ALI WAS

ARGUABLY THE GREATEST HEAVYWEIGHT BOXER OF ALL TIME, AND HE WAS CERTAINLY THE MOST FLASHY AND CHARISMATIC. IN HIS 21-YEAR PRO BOXING CAREER, THREE IN WHICH HE WAS FORCIBLY INACTIVE, ALI WON 56 FIGHTS WITH ONLY FIVE DEFEATS BEFORE RETIRING AS THE FIRST BOXER TO WIN THE HEAVYWEIGHT CHAMPIONSHIP THREE TIMES.

It was his prowess in the ring, boisterous personality, flashy showmanship, and strongly held religious and moral convictions that first made Ali a figure of deep controversy. These traits later made him a folk hero.

Born Cassius Marcellus Clay on January 17, 1942, in Louisville, Kentucky, Ali began boxing at age 12, training in a community recreation center. Instead of taking the bus to school, he ran to build his endurance and dodged rocks thrown by his brother to improve his ability to slip punches.

Ali won 100 of 105 amateur fights, capturing six Kentucky Golden Gloves and two national Golden Gloves championships before winning the Olympic light heavyweight title in 1960. Turning pro the same year, he beat 19 opponents before taking his first heavyweight title from Charles "Sonny" Liston in 1964.

Ali was a seven-to-one underdog against Liston, but that fight brought him international fame, which was bolstered by his self-promotion. Ali spouted poetry and frequently predicted, with accuracy, the round in which he would vanquish his opponents.

After the Liston fight, Ali acknowledged his religious conversion to Islam and proclaimed his name change, which helped make the Black Muslims a major religious force in America. Ali then defended his title nine times until 1967, when he refused, as a conscientious objector, to enter the draft and go to Vietnam. He was stripped of his title for three and a half years, but during this time, Ali became a worldwide symbol of moral consciousness.

After the Supreme Court reversed his draft-dodging conviction in 1971, Ali returned to the ring for a series of legendary fights. He suffered his first professional loss to "Smokin'" Joe Frazier in March 1971, trying to regain his title, but later beat Frazier twice. In the famous "Rumble in the Jungle" fight in Kinshasa, Zaire, in October 1974, Ali won his title back in a surprising eighth-round knockout of George Foreman.

After losing the title to Leon Spinks and then regaining it from him—both fights came in 1978—Ali retired from boxing in 1979. He came out of retirement for financial reasons twice, in 1980 to lose to Larry Holmes and in 1981 to lose to Trevor Berbick. Finally, a month before he turned 40, Ali hung up his boxing gloves for good.

Ali continues to make personal appearances and speeches around the country, usually speaking of his deeply held spiritual beliefs.

Facing page: *Ali boasts of his prowess in the ring.* Left: *Ali poses in March 1967, just before being stripped of his title and boxing license for refusing to be inducted in the service. He received a five-year prison sentence for his action, but the Supreme Court reversed the decision in September of 1971 and his license was restored.*

HEARING HIS CALL TO THE MINISTRY AT AGE 17, RICHARD ALLEN BECAME AMERICA'S FIRST BLACK LICENSED PREACHER AND ORDAINED DEACON. IN 1816, AFTER A SERIES OF SUCCESSFUL COURT BATTLES, HE FOUNDED THE AFRICAN METHODIST EPISCOPAL CHURCH AS AN INDEPENDENT RELIGIOUS DENOMINATION.

Richard Allen was a slave who had a religious conversion experience at the age of 17 that made him pursue the ministry as his life's work. In so doing, he became the first African American licensed to preach (1782) and the first ordained as a deacon (1799) in this country. He also founded an independent church denomination.

Allen was born on February 14, 1760, in Philadelphia, where his family was owned by Quaker lawyer Benjamin Chew. He was by all accounts a kindly master, but when Chew's law practice failed, he sold the Allen family to a Dover, Delaware, plantation owner.

Methodist preachers were active in the area. Allen heard the teachings and in 1777 converted. With his master's permission, he joined the Methodist Society, taught himself to read and write, and soon began leading the meetings. In 1781, Allen's master allowed him to purchase his freedom and he returned to Philadelphia.

During the Revolutionary War, Allen used his job as wagon driver to preach at regular stops. In 1786, he joined the mostly White St. George's Methodist Episcopal Church in Philadelphia, where he was allowed to hold separate prayer meetings for Blacks.

But one Sunday morning, Allen and some Black friends were met at the church door and directed to the upstairs gallery. When they entered the main floor anyway, they were not allowed to kneel in prayer. Allen and his group walked out. Such difficulties were becoming a growing problem for Black Methodist worshipers everywhere.

The next year, Allen and Absalom Jones organized the independent Free African Society, a beneficial and mutual aid organization. By 1794, the Society had saved enough money to build the Bethel Church, which Allen established as an independent African Methodist Episcopal (AME) congregation.

However, a legal struggle ensued between the church and the Methodist Society over control of Bethel church. But in 1816, the Pennsylvania Supreme Court ruled that Bethel could become independent of the Methodist Society.

Along with other AME congregations that had sprung up in Baltimore, Wilmington, and elsewhere, Bethel's congregation established the African Methodist Episcopal Church as an independent denomination in April 1816. The newly formed denomination consecrated Allen as its first Bishop.

Afterward, Allen opened day schools for Black students, supported moderate antislavery activities, and encouraged moral reform. He used the basement of Bethel Church to give safe haven to fugitives as they traveled the Underground Railroad. Allen also led the call for the first national Black convention to protest the assault on free Blacks launched by the American Colonization Society.

Allen and his wife, Sara, were entombed long after their deaths in that same church basement in 1901. In 1876, a monument to Allen was erected in Philadelphia's Fairmont Park—it is considered to be the first statue erected for a Black man by other Black Americans.

Facing page: *During the War of 1812, Allen, along with Absalom Jones and James Forten, enlisted about 2,500 African Americans to help build Philadelphia's defenses.* Above: *Allen worked as a master shoemaker in order to save enough money to buy a lot on which to build Bethel Church.*

MARIAN ANDERSON

MARIAN ANDERSON WAS ONE OF AMERICA'S MOST CELEBRATED SINGERS OF THE 20TH CENTURY, WITH A NEARLY THREE-OCTAVE VOICE THAT RANGED FROM LOW D TO HIGH C. SHE WAS THE FIRST AFRICAN AMERICAN TO SOLO WITH NEW YORK'S METROPOLITAN OPERA AND SHE RETIRED IN 1965 AFTER A FAREWELL CONCERT AT CARNEGIE HALL.

Known as the "baby contralto" when she sang in Philadelphia churches as a child, Marian Anderson became one of the 20th century's most celebrated singers and broke several racial barriers in American music along the way.

Anderson made history twice. In February 1939, the by-then world-famous contralto was refused permission by the Daughters of the American Revolution to sing in Constitution Hall in Washington, D.C., because of her color.

A resulting nationwide protest caused First Lady Eleanor Roosevelt to resign from the group and arrange for Anderson to give a free Easter morning concert that April on the steps of the Lincoln Memorial. A crowd estimated at 75,000 people, including government officials, Supreme Court judges, and everyday citizens, attended. She eventually sang at Constitution Hall, but not until 1953.

She made history again, however, in 1955, when she was invited to become the first African-American soloist to perform at the Metropolitan Opera House in New York. Langston Hughes called Anderson's performance as Ulrica in the Verdi opera *Un Ballo in Maschera,* "a precedent-shattering moment in American musical history." *The New York Times* deemed the breakthrough so important to the issue of race relations in America that it ran a front-page story on Anderson's debut the next morning.

Anderson was born in Philadelphia on February 27, 1902, with what she called a compulsion to make music. She ran errands for neighbors to earn enough money to buy a violin from a pawn shop and later persuaded her father to buy a piano, on which she and her sisters taught themselves to play.

But what she did most was sing. In fact, she often missed her classwork because she was often singing at nearby schools and at churches. In 1919, Anderson began studying with the famous music teacher Giuseppe Boghetti. Her church paid for the first

Facing page: *Despite Anderson's love of classical music, her passion was jazz. She was an avid collector of jazz records and she played jazz piano.* Left: *In 1939, Anderson sang at a Easter morning concert on the steps of the Lincoln Memorial, after being denied permission to sing at Constitution Hall in Philadelphia by the Daughters of the American Revolution.*

year of instruction, but after, Boghetti was so enamored that he tutored her for free for years.

In 1925, Anderson bested 300 other young singers in a competition to win a contract for concert tours. This led to her appearance with the New York Philharmonic Orchestra. From 1933 to 1935, she toured Europe on fellowships and sang for royalty in England, Sweden, Norway, and Denmark. It was during this extended excursion that the famous Arturo Toscanini called one of Anderson's concerts something you hear only once every 100 years.

Three years after her return to America, Anderson was considered one of America's leading contraltos. Her recordings were national hits and her concerts sellouts. By 1941, she was one of America's highest paid concert artists and, in 1978, received the John F. Kennedy Center for the Performing Arts Award for her "lifetime achievements in the arts." Anderson died in 1993.

LOUIS ARMSTRONG

Louis Armstrong was the father of the jazz swing movement that was popular in the early 1920s. His talent for improvisation, technical prowess, and feel for the music made him the principal model for jazz musicians of his time, and for many artists who remain popular today.

Armstrong was born in 1900, in the impoverished Storyville neighborhood in New Orleans. Raised partly by his grandmother, and later by his mother, Armstrong grew up listening to blues and ragtime played at popular neighborhood hangouts. He started singing tenor with a barbershop quartet as a teenager, then learned the bugle while sentenced to a reform school for delinquency. Eventually, he moved up to the cornet, then became bandleader at the Home for Colored Waifs. Armstrong had never touched a horn before the music teacher at the reform school handed him an alto horn in practice one day.

When Armstrong was released, he began sitting in with local bands, and later replaced legendary New Orleans cornet player King Oliver as leader of the city's most popular jazz band. From age 18 to 22, he performed in clubs and on riverboats, before moving to Chicago in 1922. There he played as second cornet in Oliver's Creole Jazz Band, a group that heavily influenced the Windy City's jazz musicians. In 1924, he moved to New York and joined Fletcher Henderson and His Black Swan Troubadours. By this time, musicians were beginning to recognize and to imitate Armstrong's innovative style.

Armstrong returned to Chicago in 1925 and began a series of recordings known as the Hot Five and Hot Seven, which revolutionized the way jazz music was performed. During this time, he switched from the cornet to the trumpet because of its brighter tone. One of the songs in that series, "Heebie Jeebies," became his first recording as a scat singer, allegedly because he dropped the music. He also perfected the so-called "swing" style of jazz, where notes are placed a fraction before or behind the beat. He also created the stop-time solo break, where the music stops for the fea-

tured player, then picks up again. His gravelly singing voice became a trademark that is still imitated today.

Armstrong then went back to New York in 1929 and became a prolific performer on stage and on screen. He was one of the first African Americans to have a sponsored radio show, and he appeared often in feature films. But some critics feel his commercial success robbed his music of the flair it once had, and most experts consider Armstrong a pop singer after the mid-1930s.

Later, the government sponsored numerous international tours for Armstrong, who became a goodwill ambassador for American music. He suffered a heart attack in 1959, and increasing health problems caused him to curtail his performances. He died July 6, 1971, in New York City.

Facing page: *The legendary Louis Armstrong popularized scat singing, perfected "swing" jazz, and created the first stop-time solo breaks during a performance.* Left: *Armstrong was known the world over as "Satchmo," short for satchel mouth. His white handkerchief, used for wiping his profusely perspiring brow, became his trademark.*

CRISPUS ATTUCKS

CRISPUS ATTUCKS CARRIED THE TORCH FOR FREEDOM AS THE FIRST MAN TO DIE IN THE HISTORIC BOSTON MASSACRE. A RUNAWAY SLAVE WHO BECAME A SAILOR AND TAUGHT HIMSELF TO READ AND WRITE, ATTUCKS WAS THE ULTIMATE SYMBOL OF THE AMERICAN BATTLE FOR INDEPENDENCE.

Crispus Attucks epitomized all that was best in colonial America. Born a slave in Massachusetts, he escaped and became an educated man. He eventually helped begin America's armed resistance against British rule. Attucks was the first to die in the Boston Massacre, and he became a beacon for the American struggle for independence.

Attucks was born a slave about 1723 (he has no known birth date), in Framingham, Massachusetts. He was the son of an African father and a Native American mother. As a child, he was repeatedly sold from one master to another, but he escaped in 1750. Attucks became a sailor and whaler, following the sea became his destiny.

The muscular mulatto learned to read and write, and he joined the American struggle for freedom from the British. Attucks attended meetings with other patriots to discuss ways to fight the burdensome taxes levied by England. He then wrote a letter of protest to Governor Thomas Hutchinson, who was the top Tory politician of the province.

According to most accounts, on March 5, 1770, Attucks spearheaded a noisy crowd of protesters who confronted a company of British soldiers stationed at the Custom House on Boston's King Street. Witnesses say Attucks led the demonstrators, who were armed with banners and clubs, and that the crowd began throwing snow and ice at the soldiers. Attucks then grabbed one British soldier's bayonet and knocked him down. The frightened soldiers fired into the crowd, leaving Attucks dead on the ground. Four others also died. The Boston *Gazette and Country Journal* for March 12, 1770, reported Attucks was killed instantly. But his death became a symbol of the Revolutionaries' struggle.

According to testimony at the later trial of the British soldiers, prosecutors said Attucks had been "assaulted with force and arms, feloniously, willfully, and of malice aforethought." But defense lawyers for the soldiers accused Attucks of not only having formed the patriots' attack party, but said "it was Attucks to whose mad behavior, in all probability, the dreadful carnage of that night is chiefly ascribed."

Facing page: *Attucks had the highest regard for personal liberty and freedom from oppression, not only for African-American slaves, but for America itself.* Left: *In 1770, leading a revolt against burdensome taxes imposed on the colonies by England, Crispus Attucks was killed by British soldiers. This made him a martyr and the American symbol of freedom during the Revolutionary War.*

After the Revolutionary War, Attucks continued to be a symbol for the fight for freedom. African-American military companies called themselves the Attucks Guards. And from 1858 to 1870, African Americans in Boston held a Crispus Attucks Day every year. By 1888, Blacks convinced city and state officials that Attucks's contributions were important enough to warrant a monument on the Boston Common. The statue bears the name of all five men who died for the cause.

The five heroes are buried in historic Granary Burying Ground, along with other famous Revolutionary War figures including John Hancock, John Adams, and Governor William Bradford of Plymouth County.

James Baldwin is perhaps the most widely read and best known African-American author of the middle 20th century. He was a prolific writer popular with both Black and White audiences worldwide.

He sensitively and honestly examined issues of race, gender, and class. And while he argued against racial injustice, Baldwin was more apt to stress the positive, life-affirming values of Black culture than to simply blast a White racist hierarchy.

Through six novels, four plays, and seven collections of essays, among his other works, Baldwin examined America's soul. His first novel, *Go Tell It on the Mountain,* is generally regarded as his best.

Released in 1953 to vast critical acclaim, it tells the story of a young Black boy's battles with his minister father over the issue of worship. He took up the same theme in *The Amen Corner,* his play about a woman evangelist, which was published in 1965. The theme is autobiographical.

Baldwin was born August 2, 1924, in Harlem, the oldest of nine children. Raised by a zealously religious minister stepfather, Baldwin preached from the revivalist pulpit from the ages of 14 to 17. But his real passion was writing. Editor of his high school newspaper, he eventually earned enough writing awards and accompanying cash prizes to move to Paris after graduation, where he lived for eight years, beginning in 1948.

While there, he had his first novel published. He then wrote a collection of well-received essays, which he compiled as *Notes of a Native Son* in 1955. In 1956, he wrote *Giovanni's Room,* the first of two novels dealing with bisexuality; the other was *Another Country* in 1962.

Baldwin returned to the states in 1957 to work in the growing Civil Rights Movement. He made the cover of *Time* magazine in 1963 as an eloquent spokesman for Black rights. His

Facing page: *Baldwin's sensitive and honest examinations of race, gender, and class distinctions make him one of the most thoughtful writers of the 20th century.* Left: *Though Baldwin's remarks delight the crowd at this 1963 meeting of the Congress of Racial Equality, he maintained that he never intended to be a Black spokesman and was only expressing his personal thoughts.*

New Yorker magazine article on the Black Muslims and parts of the civil rights struggle was published as the book *The Fire Next Time* in 1963. The next year, his important play about racial oppression, *Blues for Mister Charlie,* opened on Broadway.

In 1968, Baldwin's popular novel *Tell Me How Long the Train's Been Gone* was released. Then in 1971, *A Rap on Race* was published, detailing a conversation with anthropologist Margaret Mead about world racism. In 1974,

Baldwin enjoyed another best-seller with *If Beale Street Could Talk,* the tale of a pregnant, unmarried 19-year-old.

In 1982, after releasing more essay collections interpreting Black and White relations in the United States, Baldwin became a professor of writing and African-American history at the University of Massachusetts at Amherst. In 1987, he received the French Legion of Honor Award. Baldwin died in France later that year from cancer.

BENJAMIN BANNEKER

Benjamin Banneker was a walking contradiction to the proposed theory of his day that Blacks were mentally inferior to Whites. Considered the first Black American man of science, Banneker was a math wizard, astronomer, and inventor.

Despite having little formal education, the self-taught, voracious reader is credited with building a wooden timepiece—the first clock entirely made in America—which kept accurate time until he died. Banneker's study of astronomy and natural phenomena enabled him to write and publish a popular annual almanac from 1791 to 1802.

In his forties, after reading math books lent to him by neighbors, Banneker became proficient enough in math to solve any problems submitted to him. He even found and corrected miscalculations that the books' authors had made. This extraordinary man also wrote a treatise on bees, conducted a mathematical study on the cycle of the 17-year locust, and correctly predicted a solar eclipse in 1789.

Banneker was born outside Baltimore as a freeman on November 9, 1731. His grandmother had been a White dairymaid who came to America as an indentured servant. His grandfather was an African prince who had been her slave until she freed him. They then married.

His grandmother, Molly, began a small farm after fulfilling her service. His father, a freed slave from Guinea who married Molly's daughter, expanded the farm to 100 acres. It was on this farm that Banneker was raised and where he spent most of his life pursuing his scientific studies.

When he was young, his grandmother and mother taught him to read the Bible, primarily so he could read it to them as they relaxed in the evening. After, he bought what few books he could afford and borrowed many others. He taught himself literature, history, and math in his spare hours.

In his early twenties, Banneker built his clock, which was a testament to his mathematical wizardry. He had never seen a wooden, striking clock before, but he had seen a pocketwatch. Banneker used math ratios to determine the relationship of the gears and wheels and carved them from wood with a pocketknife. The clock operated accurately until his death more than 50 years later. It only stopped running because Banneker's house caught fire and the clock burned.

Eventually, Banneker took over the family farm, raising tobacco, wheat, and corn as cash crops. He kept a large vegetable garden for his personal use, and he collected beehives for honey, which he sold. He also learned to play flute and violin to entertain himself. After his parents' deaths, Banneker sold portions of the farm for the money that would allow him to continue his scientific studies.

A few years earlier, Banneker had befriended his neighbors, the Ellicotts, a Quaker family of surveyors and industrialists. They had lent him books on astronomy and instruments to work out calculations. After they saw his abilities, they enlisted Banneker's assistance on several projects.

When President George Washington assigned the Ellicotts to survey a 10-square-mile area that would become the new national capital of Washington, D.C., in 1790, Banneker helped them. He made calculations and used astronomical instruments for marking base points. Though 60 years old, he worked on the project for several months until they had established the baselines and initial boundaries for the new territory.

When Banneker returned to his farm, he was even more interested in astronomy. During this period and for the next ten years, Banneker made startlingly accurate studies of the stars. He published his results nationally and internationally in his popular almanacs. More than 29 editions of the almanacs were issued. He was the first to propose the establishment of a department of peace to replace the existing department of war.

Thomas Jefferson himself was a fan of Banneker's almanacs—particularly because they displayed the mental aptitude African Americans were capable of. Jefferson sent almanacs overseas to European scientists and leaders, who learned of, studied, and praised Banneker's work.

In the later part of his life, Banneker lived alone on his farm. He often entertained friends and visitors who were aware of his great repute. Banneker graciously engaged them in deep, philosophical conversations. He also became involved with the abolitionist movement, especially after the invention of the cotton gin entrenched the institution of slavery in the South in 1793.

Banneker died quietly at his home on October 9, 1806, after taking a final walk in his garden. He was 74 years old.

Facing page: *Banneker was mostly self-taught. He studied the workings of a clock to construct one himself. The clock struck the hour every hour for over 50 years.* Above: *Pictured is one of Banneker's almanacs. There were more than 29 editions issued.*

JAMES P. BECKWOURTH

An explorer, trader, and scout, James P. Beckwourth was a mountain man in the legendary tradition of pioneers who conquered the West. He discovered a pass between California and Reno that became part of a major emigrant route.

James P. Beckwourth was a tireless pioneer who helped tame the Wild West. He was one of the frontiersmen who battled an unfriendly land. The curmudgeonly but talkative man led several expeditions, including the one that opened up a barren patch of land in the Sierra Nevada Mountains. Beckwourth epitomizes the myth of an American hero.

Born in Fredericksburg, Virginia, the son of a White Revolutionary War veteran and an African-American mother with Native American blood, Beckwourth was the third of 13 children. As a child, he lived on the banks of the Missouri River. Beckwourth endured only four years of education before running away to New Orleans. But racism kept the young, ambitious man from getting a job, so in 1823, he became a scout for the Rocky Mountain Fur Company.

From there, the hardy man known for his strong legs and his ability to travel quickly became almost a legend, working for the next 13 years as a miner, guide, trapper, army scout, soldier, and hunter. Beckwourth was accepted as an equal by Native American nations, including the Blackfoot and Crow, who respected his outdoor skills. By 1842, he was fighting in the Second Seminole War, as well as on the side of other Native Americans in battles among various groups.

Beckwourth was also an entrepreneur, building and operating three trading posts nestled in the headwaters of the Arkansas and South Platte rivers. By 1840, he had established his own trading posts, first in what is now Taos, New Mexico, then later in present-day Los Angeles. But Beckwourth was caught up in the bloody battle for western land, fighting first in the California revolution against Mexico, then in the War with Mexico, where he served as a guide and dispatch carrier.

After these wars ended, Beckwourth made his final trip to California. In 1848, Beckwourth made a historic discovery while working as chief scout for the exploring expedition of General Charles Fremont. The canny frontiersman found a pass winding through the Sierra Nevada Mountains that led to the Sacramento Valley. The route, named Beckwourth Pass, later became a popular way to emigrate to California.

2 6

Facing page: *Rather than live the citified life on the East Coast, James Beckwourth, born in 1798 in Virginia, opted to travel ever westward, conquering the new frontiers of America.* Left: *Green River, Utah, was where Beckwourth hunted while he was a trapper. As "beaver waters" go, the Green River was very lucrative.*

In 1866, the U.S. government needed a liaison with the Crows, and Beckwourth was the logical choice. Beckwourth had even married into several nations, including the Crows. But some accounts say Beckwourth's devotion to his Native American friends led to his murder by those who were once enamored of his courage and strength. Reportedly, the Crows wanted Beckwourth to stay with them and restore them to their preeminence among the Native Americans. When he refused, it is said that they poisoned Beckwourth in 1886, even as they honored him with a grandiose farewell feast usually reserved for great chiefs.

MARY McLEOD BETHUNE

Mary McLeod Bethune was a beacon of hope to generations of Black youth and a tireless crusader for the African-American cause. She helped shape the formation of the Civil Rights Movement, was a friend and advisor to the Roosevelt Administration, and facilitated the distribution of federal dollars into Black education and vocational training. Bethune founded scores of schools and organizations, most notably Bethune-Cookman College and the National Council of Negro Women. She was also one of the top social activists of the New Deal years.

Bethune was born in 1875, near Mayesville, South Carolina, the fifteenth of 17 children. Bethune attended Scotia Seminary in North Carolina and what became the Moody Bible Institute in Chicago. By 1895, after failing to get a job as a missionary in Africa, she moved first to Georgia then to Florida to teach.

Believing that education was the primary route to equality for Blacks, Bethune founded the Daytona Educational and Industrial Institute for young Black women with just five students and $1.50. By using her charisma and strong belief in the project to raise money, she molded the facility into what is now Bethune-Cookman College.

But the big, dark-skinned woman with the implacable will didn't stop there. In 1924, she became president of the National Association of Colored Women. Bethune had a brilliant vision of Black women taking an active role in public affairs at a national level. By 1935, she had established the National Council of Negro Women (NCNW), an umbrella organization

Bethune listens as First Lady Eleanor Roosevelt calls for federal antilynching legislation "just as soon as possible." Mrs. Roosevelt gave the speech before the Second National Conference of Negro Youth, in 1939.

that grew to include 22 national groups with a strong lobbying presence in Washington.

The next year, Bethune took the helm of the Division of Negro Affairs for the National Youth Administration (NYA), which was an agency geared to helping young people get jobs during the Great Depression and the war effort. Bethune worked to achieve equal benefits for Blacks and Whites, lobbying for money for Black college students, and fighting to get African-American people decision-making positions in NYA and other social organizations. Her efforts finally made it possible for Blacks to get pilot training and defense department jobs.

In 1936, the strong-minded pioneer formed the Federal Council of Negro Affairs, more popularly known as the Black Cabinet, which facilitated two precedent-setting national Black conferences.

Ill health forced Bethune to cut back her activities in the 1940s, and she began writing newspaper columns for the *Chicago Defender* and the *Pittsburgh Courier.* She died of a heart attack at home in 1955. In 1974, a statue was built in her honor in Washington, D.C., the first in the capital to portray either a woman or an African American.

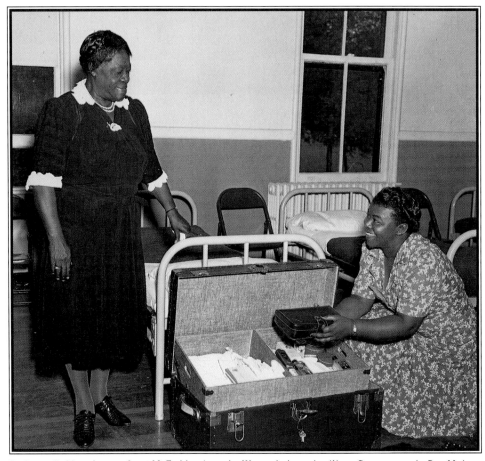

Bethune (left) welcomes Inna McFadden into the Women's Army Auxiliary Corps camp in Des Moines, Iowa, in 1942, as part of the war effort. McFadden was a new WAAC enlistee.

GWENDOLYN BROOKS

WAS THE FIRST AFRICAN AMERICAN TO WIN A PULITZER PRIZE OF ANY KIND, WHICH SHE DID IN 1950 FOR HER BOOK OF POETRY TITLED ANNIE ALLEN. BROOKS'S ESTEEMED LIFETIME BODY OF WORK AND SUPERB LANGUAGE SKILLS LED TO HER APPOINTMENT AS POET LAUREATE FOR THE STATE OF ILLINOIS.

Gwendolyn Brooks is a Pulitzer Prize-winning poet who uses her unique vision of the African-American community to focus on the rigors of urban existence, empowerment, and the flavor of street life. A muse to the Black experience and the former poet laureate of Illinois, she has more than 60 honorary degrees.

Gwendolyn Brooks started writing when she was only seven years old. Strongly influenced by writers ranging from e. e. cummings to Langston Hughes, her poetry has provided a voice for, and given a portrait of, the African-American struggle.

Her writings include award-winning poetry for both adults and children, an autobiographical novel, and short stories. A humanitarian, Brooks remains a symbol of achievement in the arts.

Brooks's poetry is praised for its technical brilliance and craftsmanship, and includes the influences of colloquial speech, spirituals and blues, in addition to traditional rhyme and sonnet forms. Writing often in free verse, Brooks has such skill with language that her work is appreciated by the most highbrow of literary critics, but is still accessible and enjoyable for the most ordinary of readers.

Brooks was born June 7, 1917, in Topeka, Kansas, the daughter of a teacher and a janitor who had once studied medicine. During her happy childhood on the streets of a south side Chicago neighborhood known as Bronzeville, Brooks learned early to appreciate education, literature, and music.

She attended predominantly White high schools and discovered that it was difficult for a quiet Black girl to fit in. A shy and somewhat lonely child, Brooks displayed a penchant for concocting rhymes as early as age seven.

By age 11, Brooks was already keeping her poems in a notebook. She studied the poetry of T. S. Eliot, Shakespeare, Ezra Pound, Paul Laurence Dunbar, and Countee Cullen. She developed a love for alliteration and the music of language. At a very early age, she decided that her life's work would be as a poet. By the age of 13, she had already been published in local newspapers and a national magazine. While in high school, Brooks sent poems to legendary Black poets

James Weldon Johnson and Langston Hughes. Hughes's enthusiasm over the writings of a 16-year-old sustained Brooks in her desire to succeed as a writer. In 1941, a modern poetry class at the South Side Community Art Center in Chicago helped hone Brooks's talent in serious poetic technique. A 1943 award from the Midwestern Writer's Conference validated her efforts.

By 1945, Brooks published her first book of poetry, *A Street in Bronzeville*, which depicted the lives of poor and working-class Blacks. The same year, she was chosen as one of America's Top Ten Women by *Mademoiselle* magazine. A review in *Poetry* at the time said her writing showed "a capacity to marry the special quality of her race with the best attainments of our contemporary poetry tradition."

Brooks received Guggenheim fellowships in 1946 and 1947, plus grants from the American Academy of Arts and Letters and the National Institute of Arts and Letters. Brooks became the first African American in the country to win a Pulitzer Prize, for her 1950 book *Annie Allen*. Some Black critics accused her of writing it for White approval. Several other books followed, including the 1953 novel *Maud Martha*, a semiautobiography

Facing page: Brooks makes an appearance at Lincoln Center's Literacy Volunteers Benefit in 1992. She has been active in the world of letters since age seven, when she first began writing poetry. Above: The former poet laureate of the state of Illinois has received numerous honors, including a Lifetime Achievement Award from the National Endowment for the Arts in 1989.

of a Black woman growing up in Chicago. The book describes Black-White relations between the period of the Depression and World War II.

Brooks changed the direction of her writing when the Black empowerment movement began in the 1960s. Her 1960 collection of poems, titled *The Bean Eaters,* marked the transition and revealed her growing consciousness about the oppression of African Americans. Her 1968 book, *In the Mecca,* examines life in Black tenements and includes odes to Malcolm X and Medgar Evers. *In the Mecca* was nominated for a National Book Award.

With *Riot,* in 1969, Brooks began publishing exclusively with Black presses. Her previous works had been published primarily by Harper's. In the early 1970s, *Aloneness, A Brookside Treasury, Jump Bad, Beckonings,* and her autobiography, *Report From Part One,* were all published by Broadside Press, the Detroit-based company owned by Detroit Poet Laureate Dudley Randall. In 1987, Brooks herself published *Blacks*, an anthology of her published works from the beginning of her career.

Brooks was chosen poetry consultant to the Library of Congress for 1985 and 1986, and she received a Lifetime Achievement Award from the National Endowment for the Arts in 1989. In 1990, she became the first scholar to hold the new Gwendolyn Brooks Distinguished Chair in the English department at Chicago State University.

Brooks continues to write and give readings of her works. She also funds promising young writers out of her own pocket and through an annual poetry contest she hosts. She lives on Chicago's South Side.

Right: At home in 1976, Brooks holds a compendium containing her greatest works, including Annie Allen, The Bean Eaters, Maud Martha, In the Mecca, *and* A Street in Bronzeville. *Facing page: Brooks became the first African American to win a Pulitzer Prize in any category in 1950 for her collection of poetry titled* Annie Allen. *At the time, she was a 32-year-old housewife, mother of a 9-year-old son, and a part-time secretary.*

ONE OF THE MOST POPULAR AND INFLUENTIAL PERFORMERS IN THE HISTORY OF AMERICAN MUSIC, JAMES BROWN IS ALSO AN ASTUTE BUSINESSMAN WHO HAS OWNED FAST-FOOD FRANCHISES, RECORD AND PUBLISHING COMPANIES, RADIO STATIONS, A BOOKING AGENCY, AND A PRIVATE JET. THE TWO-TIME GRAMMY WINNER HAS ALSO BEEN INDUCTED INTO THE ROCK AND ROLL HALL OF FAME.

Just as a dam harnesses the raging currents of water to make electricity, James Brown captured the power of raw energy, pure feeling, and infectious rhythms to become one of the most influential performers of American popular music.

It's unclear whether this dynamo was born in 1928, 1933, or 1934. But it is known that he grew up in Augusta, Georgia, in abject poverty. He did whatever he could to earn extra money—shining shoes, picking cotton, and singing gospel and pop music he learned by ear and imitation in local clubs. But when he took to crime in 1949, Brown was sentenced

to reform school, where he served three and a half years. After his release, he joined the Gospel Starlighters in 1952. The group soon became known as James Brown and the Famous Flames and they switched to rhythm-and-blues (R&B) music.

One story about how Brown got discovered was that before a Little Richard show in Toccoa, Georgia, the Flames took the stage and gave an impromptu performance. Richard's manager caught it and signed the group. However it happened, Brown's career began in 1956 with a contract with King Records.

The Flames released their first single, "Please, Please, Please," in 1956, which soon became one of Brown's signature hits. The group then began a grueling string of one-night stands across the country, where they honed their sound into razor-sharp precision.

Brown's rugged concert schedule, his insistence on rehearsing his band (which eventually grew to 40 members) until they reached his standard of excellence, and the enormous energy he expended dancing and singing earned him the title "The Hardest-Working Man in Show Business."

Brown hit the top in 1963 with his unusual, for the time, concept of recording a live performance. His *James Brown Live at the Apollo*

hit number 2 on the *Billboard* charts, and along with his 1965 single "Papa's Got a Brand New Bag," catapulted him into international superstardom in the 1960s and 1970s.

Brown was the leading proponent of "soul" music, and his songs reflected growing racial pride among African Americans. His hit "Say It Loud, I'm Black and I'm Proud" became a new Black national anthem.

His rhythmic arrangements featured tight, repetitious, almost hypnotic grooves, accented by a heavy bass line and flashy horns, with an unusual emphasis on the first beat, not the normal second and fourth. These arrangements created the foundations of funk music, which crested in the 1970s and 1980s.

Brown won a Grammy Award in 1965 for best R&B recording with "Papa's Got a Brand New Bag" and another for best R&B performance for "Living in America" in 1987. In 1986, he was inducted into the Rock and Roll Hall of Fame.

Left: *Brown uncharactiscally singing while sitting. His energetic, constantly moving stage show earned him the nickname "The Hardest-Working Man in Show Business." Right: Brown was not just a performer. He hit the charts with more than 100 songs as a writer and composer.*

WILLIAM WELLS BROWN

WILLIAM WELLS BROWN

WAS AN ESCAPED SLAVE WHO BECAME AN IMPASSIONED ABOLITIONIST, LECTURER, AND UNDERGROUND RAILROAD CONDUCTOR. IN 1853, HE BECAME THE FIRST AFRICAN-AMERICAN AUTHOR TO HAVE A NOVEL PUBLISHED. THE BOOK, CLOTEL, WAS THE STORY OF A SLAVE CHILD CONSIDERED TO HAVE BEEN FATHERED BY PRESIDENT THOMAS JEFFERSON.

William Wells Brown was a light-skinned man who apparently could have easily passed for White. He chose not to in order to fight the institution of slavery. Brown had been a slave for almost 20 years before escaping to freedom and becoming an impassioned abolitionist and precedent-setting author.

Brown wrote the first Black novel, play, travel litany, and military study of Black America. In his written work, he was detached, calm, and objective. He gave an astonishingly detailed life of a slave who held a variety of positions in his autobiography, *Narrative of William W. Brown, a Fugitive Slave,* published in 1847. That book reportedly sold more than 10,000 copies in only two years.

He was born simply as William in 1815 in Lexington, Kentucky. His father, according to his attractive mulatto mother, was the cousin of their slave owner, physician John Young. Through this bloodline, Brown claimed to be related to Daniel Boone. In 1816, Young moved to Missouri and William spent his next 19 years near St. Louis. He worked the gamut of slave positions after being hired out to more than 10 different owners. He escaped in January 1834, in Cincinnati during a trip with his last owner.

William made his escape over eight harrowing days before he happened upon and was befriended by Quaker Wells Brown, who housed the youth for two weeks while he recuperated.

Grateful for Brown's assistance, William adopted his name and departed, settling in Cleveland. He stayed there for two years where he married and began raising a family. He then moved to Buffalo, New York.

As a steamboat worker, Brown safeguarded and spirited scores of slaves to freedom in Canada by way of the Underground Railroad. In just seven months in 1842, he's credited with safely shepherding 69 passengers along the route.

A pleasant, highly intelligent man with an engaging sense of humor, Brown became a welcomed lecturer dedicated to speaking against slavery. He taught himself to read and write, and he pursued studies in English, math, history, and literature.

In 1843, Brown gave up his life as a boat steward to work full-time as an antislavery lecturer. He worked in close association with abolitionists Wendell Phillips and William Lloyd Garrison.

Brown soon gained some national renown. In 1849, he was sent to represent the American Peace Society at a Paris conference and on an extended tour to win British support against slavery.

However, while Brown was abroad, America passed the Fugitive Slave Act of 1850. This meant that he could be captured and sent back to slavery upon his return to America. Brown remained in England until 1854. He wrote and lectured until friends there raised enough money to purchase his freedom so that he could return home.

During this period, Brown reportedly traveled more than 25,000 miles, addressed more than 1,000 meetings, and learned French, German, and Latin in the process. He wrote a book on his tours of Europe, *Three Years in Europe; Or, Places I Have Seen and People I Have Met* (1852), which made him the first Black American travel writer.

In 1853 he wrote *Clotel; Or, The President's Daughter: A Narrative of Slave Life in the United States.* Though published in England, the book is the first novel written by a Black American.

Clotel focused on the sexual exploitation of female slaves. While a novel, it was no doubt based on the experiences of his mother. The president in question in the book was Thomas Jefferson, who allegedly had a number of children by his Black slave concubine, Sally Hemings. Well-received in Europe, *Clotel* caused so much furor in America that it wasn't published in its original form until 1969. It was, though, revised and republished under different titles for 14 years after Brown returned to America.

After his return to the States, Brown sensed that the country was moving toward war, and he endorsed slave uprisings. He wrote the first play published by an African American, called *The Escape; Or, a Leap for Freedom*, published in 1858.

After the Civil War, Brown devoted himself to medicine, which he had learned from his former master John Young. He also continued writing, especially about Black life. He wrote *The Black Man: His Antecedents, His Genius, and His Achievements* in 1863, and *The Negro in the American Rebellion: His Heroism and His Fidelity* in 1867.

Brown's last book was *My Southern Home: Or, The South and Its People*, written in 1880, which was about the increasingly devastating conditions under which African Americans were finding themselves. It was also a prelude to W.E.B. Du Bois's legendary work *The Soul of Black Folks*. Brown died in Boston on November 6, 1884.

Brown was remarkable because he went from slave to boat steward, speaker, novelist, historian, doctor, reformer, and sociologist, even though he wasn't able to read or write until he was in his twenties. Though he escaped from slavery, Brown was never able to settle down, moving from one cause and adventure to another until he died.

DIPLOMAT AND SCHOLAR

DIPLOMAT AND SCHOLAR

RALPH BUNCHE ACHIEVED A NUMBER OF FIRSTS AS AN AFRICAN AMERICAN: HE RECEIVED A PH.D. FROM HARVARD UNIVERSITY IN POLITICAL SCIENCE; HE HELD AN IMPORTANT POSITION IN THE STATE DEPARTMENT; HE MEDIATED A MAJOR GLOBAL CONFLICT (THE 1948 ARAB-ISRAELI WAR); AND HE WON A NOBEL PEACE PRIZE. HE WAS ALSO INSTRUMENTAL IN DEVELOPING THE CHARTER OF THE UNITED NATIONS.

After spending his youth in abject poverty, Ralph Bunche rose to become one of this country's greatest diplomats. His primary mission was to secure and maintain peace throughout the world. In the process, he helped establish the United Nations, mediated an Arab-Israeli peace accord, and was the first African American to win the Nobel Peace Prize.

Bunche was born August 7, 1904; his father was a barber in a Detroit ghetto. His parents' poor lot in life worsened after his birth. The dismal conditions they lived in caused his father and his mother to die from tuberculosis and rheumatic fever, respectively, when he was only 12.

But Bunche had shown early scholarly promise in elementary school. After moving to Los Angeles with his grandmother, he graduated from high school as class valedictorian in 1922. In 1927, he graduated from the University of California at Los Angeles summa cum laude and as a member of Phi Beta Kappa, with a degree in international relations.

His studies earned Bunche a graduate spot at Harvard University, where he received his master's degree in government in 1928 and his Ph.D. in political science in 1934. He was the first African American to earn that doctorate at Harvard.

Bunche went on to study at Northwestern University, the London School of Economics, Capetown University, and throughout Africa. He also established the Political Science Department at Howard University in Washington, D.C. Between 1938 and 1940, he collaborated with Swedish sociologist Gunnar Myrdal on *An American Dilemma*. This book was a landmark study of race relations in the United States.

During World War II, Bunche became a specialist on African affairs with the State Department, making him the first African American to hold an important position with that government branch. Afterward, he helped draw up the charter for the United Nations and developed the framework for governing the defeated countries.

Bunche earned his stripes during the 1948 Arab-Israeli War, when he became the key mediator of the conflict after the original United Nations negotiator was assassinated. Bunche secured a truce in 1949 and won the Nobel Peace Prize for that effort the next year. He dedicated the rest of his life to the United Nations, calling it the greatest peace effort in history.

A key United Nations member for two decades, Bunche rose to the post of undersecretary for special political affairs. The chief troubleshooter for resolving global unrest, his most important accomplishments involved resolving the 1956 Suez crisis, helping to end the 1960 crisis in newly independent Zaire, and directing the 1964 peacekeeping expedition to Cyprus.

Ralph Bunche retired from the United Nations in 1970 and died in New York City on December 9, 1971.

Left: *Bunche (middle) listens to United Nations Secretary General U Thant during a 1969 press conference.*
Right: *Though active in global affairs, Bunche also involved himself domestically, speaking out against racial discrimination. He participated in the Selma and Montgomery, Alabama, civil rights marches in 1965.*

MARGARET BURROUGHS

IS FOUNDER AND DIRECTOR EMERITUS OF THE DUSABLE MUSEUM OF AFRICAN AMERICAN HISTORY IN CHICAGO, THE NATION'S FIRST AND FOREMOST BLACK MUSEUM. WITH MORE THAN 50,000 ARTIFACTS, IT CONTAINS JOE LOUIS'S BOXING GLOVES AND W. E. B. DUBOIS'S GRADUATION ROBE.

Margaret Burroughs's lifelong work has been in the creation, administration, and preservation of art and Black history in all their varied forms.

Although this multitalented artist is renowned for her painting, poetry, and sculpture, her greatest claim to fame is the DuSable Museum of African American History in Chicago, which she founded in 1961 as the nation's first major, and still foremost Black museum.

Becoming keeper of the culture and heritage of a people was something Burroughs aspired to since childhood. She was born Margaret Taylor on November 1, 1917, in Saint Rose Parish, Louisiana. Her family moved north to Chicago in 1920. By the time she graduated high school in 1933, Burroughs was participating in local art fairs.

In 1937, she earned her teaching certificate for elementary grades, and in 1939, she earned her teaching certificate for upper grades, but she elected to pursue her art instead. It wasn't until Burroughs received her bachelor's degree in art education from the Art Institute of Chicago in 1946 that she combined her vocation and avocation as an art instructor at DuSable High School in Chicago, a position she held for 22 years.

In 1940, she had already become a charter member of Chicago's famed South Side Community Arts Center, which was created as part of the Works Progress Administration and dedicated by First Lady Eleanor Roosevelt. The Center was an important location for African Americans to take classes and display their art; Burroughs would remain there for 20 years as an officer and trustee. The Arts Center was the centerpiece of what Yale English Professor Robert Bone dubbed "The Chicago Renaissance," between 1945 and 1960.

Meanwhile, she exhibited her own works throughout the country, including the annual national showcase of Black art at Atlanta University. In 1947 and 1955, she won awards at the showcase for her print and watercolor works, respectively. In 1949, Burroughs married Charles Burroughs, a writer who had lived for 17 years in the Soviet Union. In the 1950s, she enjoyed international success in Mexico and Europe for her oils and acrylics.

In the late 1960s, after producing a series of works portraying great African Americans including Harriet Tubman, Crispus Attucks, and Frederick Douglass, Burroughs wrote a poem to her grandson, Eric Toller, explaining her responsibility in producing the series. Another poem, *What Shall I Tell My Chil-*

dren Who Are Black?, became nationally famous, and it refers to a collection of African-American folk expressions she had published in 1955.

In 1961, in order to "preserve, interpret and display our heritage," as Burroughs says, she opened the Ebony Museum of Negro History in her own home. Soon, she renamed the museum the DuSable Museum in honor of Chicago's first settler, a Black man. An overwhelming grassroots response caused the city to donate an old park building, which in 1968 became the permanent site of the museum.

Burroughs retired as a humanities professor at Chicago's Kennedy-King College in 1979 and has been director emeritus of her museum since 1985, when Mayor Harold Washington appointed her to the Chicago Park District Board.

Burroughs poses with a bust of Jean Baptiste Pointe DuSable, the settler and fur trader who founded the city of Chicago and after whom her DuSable Museum of African American History is named. The sculpture is by artist Marion Perkins.

GEORGE WASHINGTON *CARVER WAS A FAMOUS BLACK SCIENTIST WHO REVOLUTIONIZED FARMING IN THE SOUTH WITH HIS CROP COMBINATIONS AND NEW USES FOR PEANUTS AND SWEET POTATOES.*

Who would have guessed that a little African-American boy kidnapped from his owner's plantation and ransomed by his master in exchange for a racehorse would later revolutionize agriculture? But those were the humble beginnings for Dr. George Washington Carver. The famous African-American scientist looked at the damage America's one-crop system was doing and revolutionized farming. He developed an agriculture made for the problems of the South. This saved the South's dying farming system by introducing the right crop combinations and finding and promoting markets for them.

Carver pressed for the introduction of vegetables that did not rob soil of nitrates as cotton does. Since fertilizer was scarce, his idea of planting peanuts made sense.

Carver was born a slave, possibly in 1860 or 1861. At 13, he ventured off by himself to make his way in a troubled world. He had no money, support, or education. All he had was a dream—education at all costs. He courageously worked for his high school diploma. That whetted his appetite for higher education.

After several rejections, Carver became the first Black student at Simpson College in Iowa and at Iowa State University. He paid his tuition by opening a laundry business. In 1894, he received a bachelor's degree in agricultural science and, a few years later, a master's degree. This was the same year the Supreme Court embraced segregation with its ruling supporting the *Plessy* v. *Ferguson* decision, which declared "separate was equal" constitutionally. That same year, Carver became the first Black faculty member at his alma mater. Simpson would later award him a science doctorate.

Carver went on to make a big name for himself with his teaching and research activities. In 1896, Booker T. Washington, head of Tuskegee Institute in Alabama, offered Carver the top position in the school's agriculture department. He accepted. Carver stayed at Tuskegee, turning down royalties for his inventions and publicity, except when he could talk about Tuskegee, the school he loved. He received several lucrative job offers, including some from Henry Ford and Thomas Edison, but he preferred to stay at Tuskegee.

By 1921, when Carver appeared before the House Ways and Means Committee to discuss the many uses of the peanut, he was on the verge of becoming a nationally known scientist. He became known as the "Wizard of Tuskegee." Carver first experimented with peanuts in 1903. In a decade and a half, he developed more than 300 products, including foods, beverages, dyes, and cosmetics from the peanut. Because of Carver's testimony, the U.S. government imposed a tariff on imported peanuts, which delighted Southern peanut farmers who were producing 40 million bushels annually by 1920. Another thing that came out of Carver's appearance before the House Committee was his emergence as a folk hero. He became the subject of several biographies and a movie, and for years, he was one of a handful of African Americans ever mentioned in textbooks.

Books about Carver note his discoveries of several uses of the sweet potato, and also how he made his scientific crop knowledge accessible to the average person. Farmers

needed to understand the information about new crops in order to use it effectively. Additionally, at the suggestion of Tuskegee founder Booker T. Washington, Carver took his science show on the road in a wagon outfitted for agricultural demonstrations and exhibitions called the "Jesup Wagon."

Carver died in 1943, and he left his estate to the George Washington Carver Foundation as his unselfish way of giving back all the love, knowledge, and attention he had received.

Facing page: Carver conducts experiments at his laboratory at Tuskegee Institute.
Above: Carver and his students began experimenting with peanuts in 1903; the work resulted in peanuts becoming a huge cash crop for America's South.

SHIRLEY CHISHOLM,

AN ACTIVIST, EDUCATOR, AND FORMER PRESIDENTIAL CANDIDATE, MAY BE BEST REMEMBERED AS AMERICA'S FIRST BLACK CONGRESSWOMAN. SHE WAS ALSO THE FIRST WOMAN AND FIRST AFRICAN AMERICAN TO MAKE A SERIOUS BID FOR THE WHITE HOUSE.

Like most immigrants who came to America in the 1920s, Shirley Anita St. Hill's parents left Shirley's birthplace of Barbados to better themselves. And though life for Blacks was not easy in the United States, her parents insisted that their children would succeed despite the obstacles. They did decide, though, to send the children back to Barbados to live with their grandmother in 1928.

Chisholm and her sisters returned to live with their parents in 1934. Shirley, the oldest, always seemed to stand out. She expressed herself forcefully and clearly even when her

parents did not want her to. Meanwhile, this outspoken little girl excelled in her Brooklyn school just as she had in the demanding one back in Barbados. She was offered scholarships to Vassar and Oberlin colleges but instead stayed in more affordable Brooklyn.

With an education degree from Brooklyn College, Chisholm taught nursery school while she took courses at Columbia University toward her master's degree in early childhood development. She never lost sight of her aspirations; Chisholm continued to work to prove to men and to White America that women and African Americans were as capable as anyone. She fought against racism and sexism her whole life.

She married Jamaican private investigator Conrad Chisholm in 1949. Their life together was good, but Shirley continued to show her concern for her friends and neighbors in her Brooklyn community. She started day-care centers for working mothers. Her biographer, Toyomi Igus, pointed out in the 1991 book *Great Women in the Struggle,* "The centers were so successful that Brooklyn residents chose her to represent them in the New York State legislature in 1964." Four years later, Chisholm was chosen to represent them in Congress, becoming the first African-American congresswoman. She served seven terms, from 1968 to 1982, and was elected using the slogan "Unbought and Unbossed," which later would be the title of her first autobiography. (*The Good Fight,* published in 1973, was her second autobiography).

Chisholm was always an advocate for the dispossessed and the disenchanted, and always a champion for the poor. She wanted poor people to have the same opportunities other Americans had. So in 1972, Chisholm looked at the political landscape and did not see anyone representing the interests that she held so dear. She decided the only person powerful enough to become president was herself, so she threw her hat into the ring. She campaigned to win the Democratic nomination. She lost. But to many women, African Americans, and poor people, Chisholm won their hearts and earned their respect by becoming a role model.

Left: *In a wide-open presidential election year in 1972, Chisholm decided the country might just give credence to a Black, female candidate. She tossed her hat in the ring. Here she speaks at the Democratic Convention.* Right: *Chisholm flashes a victory sign after defeating civil rights leader James Farmer to become the first female Black member of Congress in 1968.*

BILL COSBY, COMEDIAN *AND TELEVISION PERSONALITY, IS ONE OF THE FUNNIEST, HIGHEST-PAID ENTERTAINERS IN AMERICA. AN AWARD-WINNING HUMORIST, COSBY HAS RECORDED MORE THAN 27 ALBUMS AND WAS THE FIRST AFRICAN AMERICAN TO STAR IN A NETWORK TELEVISION DRAMA SERIES.*

Bill Cosby started trying out comedy routines while bartending to make ends meet in college. He's now one of the top earners in the business, earning $95 million in 1989 according to *Forbes* magazine. Cosby is well known to television audiences, both through award-winning sitcoms and his neighborly mugging with children in commercials. His life is a success story that has become a beacon for many African-American comedians trying to follow in his footsteps.

William Henry Cosby was born July 12, 1937, in Germantown, Pennsylvania. He dropped out of high school to become a Navy medic. Cosby later enrolled at Temple University, where he played football and tended bar at night. Pleased with his success at entertaining customers, the tall, distinguished-looking man with the expressive face left Temple in 1962 to try his hand in local clubs.

Cosby quickly moved up to shows in New York's legendary Greenwich Village. Audiences were thrilled, and within two years Cosby was performing at some of the nation's top comedy clubs. He also became a fixture on television variety shows and guest hosted for Johnny Carson on *The Tonight Show.* In 1965, Cosby made history as the first African American to get a network television drama show, *I Spy* with Robert Culp. *The Bill Cosby Show* followed in 1969, as well as appearances on the top-rated children's show *The Electric Company.*

Cosby appeared in several hit movies, including *Uptown Saturday Night,* in the 1970s, and he returned to the silver screen in the 1980s and 1990s with features such as *Ghost Dad.* The charming, expressive comedian also became popular at ritzy clubs in Reno, Las Vegas, and Lake Tahoe. However, some of Cosby's best work has been in television commercials, particularly the ongoing series of vignettes with children produced for Jell-O.

Cosby's earnings skyrocketed after five years as star and producer of *The Cosby Show,* a television sitcom focused on the antics of an upper-middle class African-American family. The positive values and the message that Blacks can attain wealth and social status while retaining their cultural identity was a powerful one in the African-American community.

Cosby also shows a strong commitment to education with memberships in various civil rights groups, including Operation PUSH and the NAACP, plus his activities with the United Negro College Fund. In 1977, Cosby went back to school, earning a master's degree, then a doctorate in education from the University of Massachusetts at age 39. In the late 1980s, he donated $20 million to Spelman College, a Black women's facility in Atlanta.

Cosby continues performing across the country and lives in rural New England with his wife, Camille. They have five children.

Left: *In May 1966, Bill Cosby, shown with his wife, Camille, received an Emmy award for Best Actor in a dramatic TV series for his work on* I Spy. *Right: Cosby's real gift to the world has been his gentle humor and likeable nature.*

Martin Robinson Delany spent his life championing the cause of African-American empowerment, freedom, and self-elevation. Delany was an editor, author, physician, doctor, colonizationist, and Black nationalist. He attempted to create a self-governing African-American state in Africa, believing that emigration was the only way to keep Blacks away from the scourge of racism.

Delany was born in May of 1812 in Charlestown, West Virginia, the son of a slave and a free Black woman. Early on, his African grandfathers, one a Mandingo prince and the other a Golah village chieftain, regaled the young Delany with grand tales of his homeland. Delany and his four siblings learned to read from a Yankee peddler, causing such consternation among their White neighbors that the family fled to Pennsylvania.

At 19, Delany moved to Pittsburgh, studying medicine briefly and getting involved with the Anti-Slavery Society and the Underground Railroad. He married Catherine Richards and they named their seven children after prominent African Americans. Delany was an advo-

cate for Black self-reliance through education, labor, and property ownership, but he needed a venue to sow his views among the people, so he published a weekly called *The Mystery*. In 1847, he and Black abolitionist Frederick Douglass cofounded and coedited *The North Star* in Rochester, New York. Douglass once said of Delany, "I thank God for making me a man simply, but Delany always thanks him for making him a Black man."

In 1850, Delany was accepted to Harvard Medical School, but left after just one term when White students protested his admission to professors. Despite limited training, he returned to Pittsburgh a practicing physician and helped the city through a deadly cholera epidemic in 1854.

The enactment of the Fugitive Slave Act, which Delany saw as a threat to the security of African Americans across the country, made him decide that perhaps Blacks would be safest elsewhere. Delany then published *The Condition, Elevation, Emigration and Destiny of the Colored People of the United States, Politically Considered (1852)*, which listed

*A **TIRELESS FIREBRAND**, MARTIN R. DELANY WAS AN EDITOR, DOCTOR, ARMY OFFICER, AND BLACK NATIONALIST WHO SPENT HIS LIFE FIGHTING FOR AFRICAN-AMERICAN SELF-RELIANCE AND A DYNAMIC VISION OF BLACK POWER.*

Black achievements, blasted abolitionists for not fighting harder for Blacks' rights, and advocated emigration as a solution to discrimination. "We are a nation within a nation. We must go from our oppressors," Delany wrote. He continued fighting for a Black independent nation for the rest of his life.

Delany moved to Canada, then in 1859 led an investigation into the Niger River Valley in West Africa as a possible place for a Black state. He returned to the United States in 1861. After the Emancipation Proclamation in 1863, he enlisted as a medical officer in the Civil War and became the first Black Army field major, recruiting ex-slaves for regiments in South Carolina.

Delany wrote *Principals of Ethnology* in 1879, tracing Black history from biblical times. Unable to realize his dream of a free Black American state in Africa, Delany died in 1885 in Ohio, still advocating his beliefs in pride of self and the race.

Left: *Delany, the first African-American field major in the United States Army, felt that Blacks should return to Africa and create their own state.* Right: *This anonymous painting of Delany being "promoted on the battlefield for bravery," hangs in the National Portrait Gallery of the Smithsonian Institution.*

Originally a blues musician of some renown, Thomas Dorsey eventually worked exclusively within a religious setting and elevated gospel music into a nationally recognized art form. Dorsey wrote more than 1,000 songs—dozens of which have become classics—as one of the genre's most prolific composers.

Born July 1, 1899, in Villa Rica, Georgia, Thomas, the oldest child in the Dorsey family, was raised in a religious household. He played piano during the revival services of his father, a traveling Baptist preacher.

But as a youth, he was strongly influenced by blues pianists around Atlanta. To help support his family, Thomas began playing blues piano in area saloons at the tender age of 11 under the stage name "Georgia Tom." In 1916, he moved to Chicago to study at the Chicago College of Composition and Arranging and earned a reputation in the city's blues and jazz club circuit.

In the early 1920s, Dorsey performed with several jazz groups, including the Whispering Serenaders. His own Wildcats Jazz Band toured with popular blues singer Ma Rainey until 1928. Dorsey had several of his blues compositions, notably "Riverside Blues," recorded by major jazz musicians such as Joseph "King" Oliver. He also toured with legendary blues guitarist Tampa Red, with whom he composed and recorded several songs, including "Tight Like That" and "Terrible Operation Blues."

But, sticking to his upbringing in sacred music, Dorsey continued to write religious

In this 1929 photo, when Dorsey was making it big on the blues and jazz circuits, he was the cool cat known as "Georgia Tom."

compositions. In 1921, his song, "Someday, Somewhere" was included in the National Baptist Convention's *Gospel Pearls* Collection.

In the late 1920s, Dorsey turned his focus exclusively toward gospel, combining the spirituality of his lyrics with blues melodies and rhythms, which were not initially accepted in area churches because of their secular sound.

But in 1931, Dorsey experienced a personal tragedy when he lost his wife and daughter in childbirth, an experience that caused him to write "Take My Hand, Precious Lord," which has become a gospel standard and Dorsey's most famous work.

In the same year, Dorsey formed the world's first gospel choir at Ebenezer Church in Chicago and opened the first publishing company dedicated exclusively to the sale of gospel music. In 1932, he became the lifelong choir director of Chicago's Pilgrim Baptist Church and, along with gospel legend Sallie Martin, founded the National Convention of Gospel Choirs and Choruses to train gospel vocal groups and soloists.

Dorsey presided over that organization for 40 years, and for the same period, toured the country extensively with gospel caravans, both performing and lecturing. He remained active in promoting gospel music around the country until his death in Chicago on January 23, 1993, at the age of 93.

Personal tragedy caused Dorsey to write "Take My Hand, Precious Lord."

FREDERICK DOUGLASS

The fight against slavery is best exemplified by the words and deeds of one man—Frederick Douglass. In the years that spanned the abolitionist movement, Civil War, Reconstruction, and the post-Reconstruction period, Douglass championed the cause of all oppressed people. The rocklike Douglass's preeminence as race leader was to persist until his death in 1895, the very year Booker T. Washington was thrust into the role of the nation's most famous Negro by his celebrated Atlanta Compromise address, "signaling a strategic retreat with a changed national attitude," wrote Richard Bardolph in his 1959 *The Negro Vanguard.*

Douglass was born in one of the darkest periods of slavery on a plantation owned by Colonel Lloyd of Talbot County, Maryland, the White man who raped his mother. When Douglass was an infant, he was snatched from his mother and put under his grandmother's care. According to Douglass, hunger was his constant companion. "He used to run races against the cat and the dog to reach the bones that were tossed out of the window, or to snap up the crumbs that fell under the table," said his biographer, J. A.

Rogers in his 1947 *World's Great Men of Color.* Douglass would later be beaten for sneaking away to get meat.

At age eight, two years after his mother died at a neighboring estate, young Douglass was sent to live with the Auld family, where his life's ambition to learn how to read was fulfilled. Not knowing it was against the law, Mrs. Auld gave him reading lessons. Her husband scolded her when he found out, causing her to stop her literacy crusade. Douglass continued his lessons on his own, grabbing scraps of newspapers, bank notes, or any piece of paper with writing on it to teach himself.

After a series of severe thrashings for fighting and organizing slave revolts, 21-year-old Douglass plotted his 1838 escape. He somehow got hold of a sailor's uniform and a passport and climbed on a ship and sailed. The next day, he arrived in New York where he found work shoveling coal. He took on the last name of Douglass after the hero in Walter Scott's *Marmion,* married a freed woman, Anna Murray, and increased his desire to help those still in bondage by reading *The Liberator,* published by famous abolitionist William Lloyd Garrison.

Facing page and left: *After some early lessons in reading by the plantation owner's wife, Douglass taught himself how to read and write by finding any piece of paper with writing on it to practice reading. In fact, he took his last name from a character in the novel* Marmion *by Sir Walter Scott.*

Facing page: *One of Douglass's greatest skills was oration. Douglass spoke at antislavery meetings and was able to make his audience see the pain and hardship that slavery subjected people to. His speeches were so famous that when he went to England he was asked to address the Parliament.*

Three years later, he found himself in front of a crowd speaking forcefully against slavery in an antislavery meeting in Nantucket. He had the uncanny ability to transport his audiences to Slave Row. Historian Lerone Bennett said, "He could make people *laugh* at a slave owner preaching the duties of Christian obedience; could make them *see* the humiliation of a Black maiden ravished by a brutal slave owner; could make them *hear* the sobs of a mother separated from her child. Through him, people could cry, curse and *feel;* through him they could *live* slavery."

In 1845, he published his first autobiography, *Narratives of the Life of Frederick Douglass, An American Slave,* which put slavers on his track after the book had huge sales and subsequent controversy. Douglass prepared to flee to England. On his getaway boat, he made a speech so fiery that Southerners nearly killed him by throwing him overboard. His life was saved by crew members. This event garnered huge publicity in England. Lords, ladies, and earls welcomed him to their suburban estates. The now famous baritone orator, with his impressive mane of hair, addressed the Parliament. After 19 months in Great Britain, English friends gave him $2,175, of which he used $750 to buy his freedom.

His liberty now purchased, Douglass went to Rochester, New York, and started his antislavery paper, *The North Star,* and later *Frederick Douglass' Paper.* He wrote his second autobiography, *My Bondage and My Freedom,* in 1855. He returned to this form 26 years later and wrote *The Life and Times of Frederick Douglass.* The most important aspect of his writing is that it crystallized the abolition movement and mobilized both Blacks and Whites to fight slavery. A secondary result of these stellar works was the stimulation of Black scholarship; they created an audience for slave narratives and Black literary and historical works.

In his words and deeds, Douglass challenged liberals, who felt he should merely "stick to the facts" in his oratory and "leave the philosophy to them." He challenged conservatives who thought they were empowered by God to enslave Black people. And he fought both Whites and Blacks who thought his terse verse did not fit into the commonly held notions of what a Black man should be and say. In essence, Douglass challenged himself and his people to be all they could be and not let any obstacle stand in their way. He taught everyone that freedom is never free—it comes with struggle.

CHARLES RICHARD DREW

CHARLES RICHARD DREW

WAS A BRILLIANT DOCTOR WHO

PIONEERED THE USE OF BLOOD

PLASMA AND CREATED THE

WORLD'S FIRST BLOOD BANK.

DREW ALSO FOUGHT TO INCREASE

THE MEDICAL ESTABLISHMENT'S

RESPECT FOR AFRICAN-AMERICAN

PHYSICIANS, AND TO MAKE IT

EASIER FOR THEM TO WORK AT

WHITE MEDICAL FACILITIES.

Dr. Charles Richard Drew not only revolutionized the medical profession by developing a way to store blood and plasma, he also created the world's first blood bank. But Drew had another priority—crusading to change the way African Americans, especially as physicians, were viewed and treated by Whites.

Born the eldest of five children on June 3, 1904, Drew lived in the racially mixed Foggy Bottom neighborhood of Washington, D.C. The area was an enclave where Blacks rarely had to deal with the federally sanctioned Jim Crow laws. Drew was an exceptional student and athlete at Dunbar High School. He decided to become a doctor after his sister died of tuberculosis in 1920. After graduating from Amherst College in Massachusetts, Drew taught for two years, then went to McGill University in Montreal, Canada, for medical school.

While Drew served his medical internship at the Royal Victoria Hospital in Montreal, he saved an elderly man who needed a blood transfusion in order to have his leg amputated. During that time, many people died because doctors had to match the blood type before a transfusion could take place. Drew's research changed all that.

In 1935, Drew taught and practiced at Freedmen's Hospital at Howard University, where he invented a way to separate plasma from whole blood, making it possible to store blood for a week instead of just two days. More research turned up a bigger revelation: Transfusions could be performed with plasma alone, negating the need for blood typing since plasma contains no red blood cells. In 1938, Drew got a fellowship in blood research at New York City's Columbia Presbyterian Hospital and ran its first blood bank.

In 1940, Drew became the first African American to earn an advanced doctor of science degree, and he invented a technique for long-term plasma storage. He set up the world's first blood bank in Britain that same year, as part of the country's World War II effort. As America prepared to enter the war, Drew was appointed medical director of the American Red Cross's National Blood Bank program. But the U.S. War Department issued an edict forbidding the armed forces to mix Black and White blood, even while admitting in a memorandum that their decision was based on "reasons not biologically convincing, but which are commonly recognized as psychologically important in America." A furious Drew called a press conference, asking, "How have we, in this age and hour, allowed once again to creep into our hearts the dark myths and wretched superstitions of the past? . . . Will we ever share a common brotherhood?" Drew resigned his post.

In April of 1941, Drew was certified as a surgeon by the American Board of Surgery. He then returned to Howard University as a full professor. Two of his students became the first Howard graduates to qualify for the American Board of Surgery, and Drew continued pushing his students to seek internships and residencies in White establishments. His efforts greatly increased the number of Blacks getting jobs outside the African-American medical community.

Drew was appointed chief of staff at Freedman's Hospital in 1944, and was awarded the Springarn Medal by the NAACP. In 1947, Drew began an unsuccessful crusade against the American Medical Association for a policy that effectively kept Blacks from joining. The AMA didn't change its policy until 1968. (In 1996, the AMA elected its first African-American president, Dr. Lonnie R. Bristow.) Drew was later named consultant to the surgeon general of the U.S. Army.

By 1950, despite an international reputation, Drew remained poor, since Black medical researchers made far less money than private practitioners of any race. He died the morning of April 1, 1950, when he fell asleep while driving to a medical conference at Tuskegee. Drew, despite a blood transfusion at the hospital, died of internal injuries. He was 45.

Drew's outstanding work with blood has revolutionized medical surgery and saved countless numbers of lives. He found a way to separate out the plasma, which allowed for longer storage of blood. He was given the NAACP's Spingarn Medal in 1944 for his efforts.

William Edward Burghardt Du Bois was born poor in 1868 in Great Barrington, Massachusetts, but rose from his meager roots to become the brightest Black mind in the 20th century.

Showing remarkable brilliance even as a youth, W.E.B. Du Bois won scholarships that took him through Fisk and Harvard universities. He earned his master's and doctorate degrees from Harvard, and later studied at the University of Berlin.

His first works of importance included *The Suppression of the Slave-Trade of the United States of America, 1638–1870*, published in 1896, and *The Philadelphia Negro; A Social Study*, published in 1899. The latter is a classic about the social conditions of turn-of-the-century Blacks in that city. He wrote several reports about Atlanta a few years later, from 1899 to 1913, with Atlanta University. These social studies were published for the university's Conferences for the Study of Negro Problems. During this same stormy period when Whites' hostility against Blacks reached a fever pitch, DuBois also wrote the oft-quoted classic *The Souls of Black Folk*, which identified the principal problem of the 20th century as the color line.

His uncompromising opposition to injustice and Jim Crow impelled him to write scathing reports about the Atlanta Riots of 1906 and found the Niagara Movement. He later cofound the National Association for the Advancement of Colored People, which demanded full citizenship for Blacks. DuBois became the NAACP's chief spokesman through the editorship of *The Crisis* magazine. During his stint as editor, Du Bois greatly advanced African-American literature by editing many of the important voices of the Black arts revival known as the Harlem Renaissance.

Through his moving editorials, he was to stir the emotions and awaken the sense of outrage in both Blacks and Whites—an act that would draw the ire of Booker T. Washington, the more accommodationist Black leader at the time. Washington said Du Bois was an agitator who was always stirring up trouble. Du Bois said Washington's strategy would perpetuate

Left: *One of the brightest intellectual minds of the 20th century, W.E.B. Du Bois was a scholar, educator, writer, editor, and orator.* Above: *Du Bois testifies before the Senate Foreign Relations Committee against the United Nations charter in 1945. He believed the proposed charter would not protect people who were under colonial rule.*

Above: *Du Bois, leader of the American delegation, addresses the Congress of Partisans of Peace in Paris on April 22, 1949.* Facing page: *Du Bois in 1951 with his fiancée, Shirley Graham.*

civic equality, and education of the youth. One of DuBois's most often quoted philosophies was the "talented tenth." It said that Blacks' salvation will come through the accomplishments of its elite.

Hardly modest about his own achievement in defining and transcending caste and class in this country, Du Bois boasted in his autobiography, *Dusk of Dawn*: "I was the main factor in revolutionizing the attitude of the American Negro toward caste."

Du Bois had a universal outlook. He was concerned, as was Garvey, with the treatment of the darker people of other lands. In 1909, he began thinking of creating an "Encyclopedia Africana." He finally did work on it in his later years in self-imposed exile in Ghana. He was also an organizer of the Pan-African Congress, which brought together for the first time influential Blacks from Europe, Africa, and America. The first conference was held in Paris in 1919.

Du Bois traveled to the Soviet Union in the 1930s, praising the communist nation as being virtually free of racial discrimination. Ironically, he left the Communist Party, which he joined much later in 1961, in America because he felt they discounted Blacks with the Party's insistence that class and not race was the

oppression. Their debate was legendary, and to this day represents the fight between accommodationist versus the integrationist schools of thought within the African-American community. Du Bois was also critical of Black nationalist Marcus Garvey. Their conflict symbolized the differences of integrationist and Black nationalist schools of thought.

Throughout Du Bois's life, including periods when he embraced Pan-Africanism, socialism, and communism, he believed in three basic goals for Blacks: the right to vote, problem. Nevertheless, like other Blacks such as Paul Robeson and Langston Hughes, Du Bois would be harassed by the United States government for his views on the Soviet Union. Many were shocked in 1950, therefore, when he ran for the United States Senate on the American Labor Party ticket.

Du Bois's universal outlook led to him being one of the few influential African Americans associated with the founding of the United Nations. Like his colleagues Ralph Bunche and Mary McLeod Bethune, who were also U.N. cofounders, Du Bois linked the struggle of Africans with that of African Americans—another reason why many Whites and some Blacks criticized him. This resentment and harassment made him increasingly isolated. In 1963, he became a citizen of Ghana, and when he died, on August 27, 1963, he was buried in Accra, Ghana.

In addition to being one of this century's most important thinkers, Du Bois was also an important writer. Two of his works include *Black Reconstruction* (1935), which submitted the Civil War to Marxist analysis and argued the heroic role Blacks played in the conflict; and his autobiography, *Dusk of Dawn* (1940), in which he used his life as a metaphor for the race's continuing struggle.

PAUL LAURENCE DUNBAR

Paul Laurence Dunbar was a brilliant, popular poet, beloved by the Black community, whose experiences he put into lyrical language. He was one of the first Black poets to become nationally recognized by White America.

Even early on, Dunbar was seen as a Black prodigy in a White world. He was the only African American in his Dayton, Ohio, high school class, but immensely popular. In his senior year, he was elected president of the literary society and served as editor of the school newspaper.

Dunbar wanted to go to college, but did not have the resources. He was born in Dayton on June 27, 1872, to ex-slave parents. His father died when Dunbar was only 12 and there were other children to support.

So Dunbar took one of the few jobs available to a young Black man at the time, operating an elevator. He continued writing poems and sending them off to publications.

In 1893, he paid to have 56 poems published in a slim volume called *Oak and Ivy,* which he sold to his captive audience of elevator passengers. Thinking there would be opportunities at the World's Fair of 1893, Dunbar moved to Chicago, where he became Frederick Douglass's clerical assistant.

In 1895, Dunbar was able to pay to publish a second collection of his verses, called *Majors and Minors,* which presented poems he had written in standard English and in Black dialect. The book became his major breakthrough after being favorably reviewed by William Dean Howells, reigning literary critic of the day for *Harper's Weekly.*

Howells encouraged Dunbar to take the best poems from his two books and reissue them in 1896 under the title *Lyrics of Lowly Life,* for which Howells wrote the preface. The book made Dunbar a star in White literary circles and gave him the financial security to write full-time.

Offers streamed in from prestigious magazines and publishers for anything that came from his pen and Dunbar didn't disappoint, turning out a great volume of work including four novels, four volumes of short stories, and three more books of poetry.

But because of the necessity of surviving financially in the literary world, Dunbar compromised his art. He wrote uninspired prose and poems in Black dialect, which his readers seemed to prefer, instead of his preference for verse in standard English. So, despite his success, Dunbar was riddled with disappointment that his greatest talent had gone unappreciated.

However, when Dunbar died from tuberculosis on February 9, 1906, at the age of 33, the American public still considered him the dean of Black poets.

Dunbar wrote until the very end, releasing the poetic collections Lyrics of Love and Laughter *in 1903,* The Heart of Happy Hollow *in 1904, and* Lyrics of Sunshine and Shadow *in 1905. A final complete collection of Dunbar's poems was released in 1913, seven years after his death.*

KATHERINE DUNHAM

KATHERINE DUNHAM

POPULARIZED AFRO-CARIBBEAN DANCE THROUGHOUT THE WORLD AND ELEVATED BLACK DANCE INTO A SERIOUS, ACCEPTED ART FORM. AFTER STUDYING NATIVE DANCE IN AFRICA AND THE WEST INDIES, DUNHAM DEVELOPED A NEW TECHNIQUE CALLED "DANCE-ISOLATION," WHICH INVOLVED MOVING ONE PART OF THE BODY WHILE OTHER PARTS REMAINED MOTIONLESS.

Katherine Dunham, the choreographer who introduced and popularized Afro-Caribbean dance throughout the world, was also the cultural pioneer who propelled Black dance into a serious art form accepted by mainstream America.

Dunham was so serious about learning and establishing this medium as "art" that she majored in anthropology in college—all the way through the doctoral level—to study the original African and West Indian dance forms in their native environments.

Dunham herself was a mini-United Nations of mixed African, American Indian, French-Canadian, and Madagascan heritage. She was born June 22, 1909, in Chicago, Illinois, and exhibited an early interest in athletics and music, which merged into her natural talent for dance.

At the age of 15, Dunham organized a cabaret party to raise funds for her church. At the age of 21, she had started a dance school, which folded from lack of funding. But she soon joined the Negro Dance Group, where she learned ballet and mime and was allowed to teach her own pupils what she knew of African tribal dance.

After Dunham trained 150 young dancers for a program at the 1934 Chicago Century of Progress Exhibition, she received a Rosenwald Foundation grant through Northwestern University to visit Jamaica, Martinique, Trinidad, and Haiti to study the origins of the people and their dances. She later received a Guggenheim Fellowship to continue her studies and eventually received a B.A. and M.A. from the University of Chicago, and a Ph.D. from Northwestern University in anthropology.

Dunham's first ballet, *L'Ag'Ya*, based on a fighting dance from Martinique, was accepted by the Federal Theater Project of the Works Progress Administration. It was performed with success in Chicago in 1939. A year later, Dunham established her first ensemble, the Katherine Dunham Dance Company, which opened at New York's Windsor Theater with Dunham's own work,

Tropics and Le Jazz Hot. The piece was a huge success.

Shortly thereafter, the Dunham Dance Company was asked to take part in the all-Black musical *Cabin in the Sky,* with Dunham playing the role of Georgia Brown. The production had a long run, after which Dunham appeared in *Stormy Weather* and choreographed *Pardon My Sarong* and *Windy City.*

In 1943, she was guest artist for the San Francisco Symphony Orchestra and in 1945, she was guest artist for the Los Angeles Symphony Orchestra. Over the next 20 years, Dunham and her dance troupe visited almost every country in the world.

Dunham gave her last dance performance at the Apollo Theater in 1965. Afterward, she established the Performing Arts Training Center, now called the Katherine Dunham Center for the Performing Arts, at Southern Illinois University in East St. Louis, Illinois. She is now retired.

Left: *Dunham poses for publicity shots for the movie* Casbah. *She interrupted a popular six-month tour of Mexico to take the part in the movie.* Right: *Posing with her dance partner Vanoye Aike, Dunham gets ready for a new stage show in Paris in 1959.*

JEAN BAPTISTE POINTE DuSABLE

Jean Baptiste Pointe DuSable founded the settlement of Chicago in 1772. DuSable epitomized the forbearance and spirit of early African Americans, whose accomplishments represent the incredible diversity of the African-American experience.

The details of DuSable's early life are based on much conjecture, but he is believed to have been born in St. Marc, Haiti, in 1745. He was a free Black of African heritage. Since many free Blacks in Haiti were educated in France it is possible that DuSable, too, was educated there. He became a strong patriot for his country. DuSable then moved to New Orleans and ran his father's business there. The Spanish occupied Louisiana in 1764, and DuSable fled with an associate for French-controlled areas along the upper Mississippi River.

During this time, DuSable created what became a lifelong connection with several Native American nations, most notably the Potawatomie. The handsome frontiersman spent four years (1765–1769) trading furs with the Indians in St. Louis, then moved farther north into their territory, on land controlled by the English and Spanish. He lived at that time with a boyhood friend, Jacques Clemorgan, another Haitian who had received large land grants in return for doing favors for the Spanish Government.

DuSable, who remained faithful to the French, left to live among the Potawatomies. His fur trapping expeditions took him across North America, to the sites of what are now Chicago, Detroit, and Ontario, Canada.

DuSable was described in the "Recollections" of Augustin Grignon, of Butte des Morts, Wisconsin, as "a large man.... He was a trader, pretty wealthy, and drank freely." Others who knew him described him as "venerable, about six feet in height, with a well-formed figure and very pleasant countenance." DuSable was described by many as a respectable man.

In 1772, DuSable established a historic fur trading post on the Chicago River near Lake Michigan, the first permanent settlement in the area. He bought land and built his house on the north bank of the Chicago River, just where the waterway turned south, on a head of sand that extended between the river and Lake Michigan. The ambitious businessman lived a prosperous life with his Native American wife, Catherine, and their daughter, Suzanne.

The first child born in Chicago was born on his property, which also hosted the city's first marriage, and housed its first court and post office. He traded heavily with the Native Americans in the area and became known for acting as peacemaker between various warring tribes.

During the Revolutionary War, DuSable seems to have tried to play a role as peacemaker, but his intentions were questioned by both sides. DuSable was jailed on suspicion of treason by British Colonel Arent de Peyster, who described DuSable as "a handsome Negro, well-educated and settled at Eschikagou." His captor, a Lieutenant Bennett, reported that DuSable had many friends who gave him good character references. DuSable was freed after proving that he was a citizen of the United States.

DuSable later served as liaison officer between White officials and the Indian nations in the Port Huron area on the St. Clair River. He was appointed by the government at the Native Americans' request.

After acquiring and developing an 800-acre property in Peoria, DuSable returned to Chicago in the early 1780s, creating a trading post and home that became legendary for its elaborate furnishings and modern conveniences. DuSable's business was so prosperous that it included two barns, a mill, a bake

house, a poultry house, and large livestock holdings.

By 1800, DuSable sold his post to a French trader and moved to Missouri with his old friend Clemorgan. He later moved to St. Charles, Missouri, with his granddaughter and her husband. He was possibly disappointed over his defeat in an election to become chief of the Native American nations in the Mackinac area. DuSable spent most of his time hunting and fishing. Even though his holdings brought the then-unheard of sum of $1,200, DuSable died a pauper in 1818, apparently forsaken by his relatives. Still, his life and perseverance stand as a symbol of African-American ingenuity and self-reliance.

Above: *A view of what DuSable may have seen when he decided to settle in Chicago. DuSable realized that the waterway he settled on would be a strategic location from which to capitalize on trade throughout the surrounding areas. He was Chicago's first businessman, and Chicago has since become the Black business capital of America.*

No one played like him. No one arranged music like him. No one loved life like him. And no one, absolutely no one, wrote songs like him. He was one of a kind. While he was born to common parents at the turn of the century, Edward Kennedy Ellington enriched millions worldwide, earning him an eternal place among royalty. Long live the Duke!

His dad, James Edward, was a well-heeled butler and caterer who lived like a king despite his meager means. His mother, Daisy, had the confidence of a queen, despite living in segregated Washington, D.C., where separate was never equal.

After hearing a terrific pianist named Harvey Brooks in Philadelphia during a summer trip with his parents, Edward decided the musician's life was for him. It was around this time that this well-mannered, fancy-dressing, popular piano-playing boy got his royal nickname—Duke.

By the time he was 22, Duke was already a successful pianist and bandleader. He married Edna Thompson, a pianist who schooled Duke on piano and music theory when they were both still in high school. They had a son, Mercer, in 1919, who followed in his dad's footsteps.

Duke's big break came in the 1920s when he auditioned for Harlem's Cotton Club. During the Cotton Club era, the flamboyant Duke Ellington Orchestra made nationwide radio broadcasts from the club and recorded "Black and Tan Fantasy."

The Duke Ellington Orchestra soon became the first Black musicians featured at Carnegie Hall and among the first prominently featured in major motion pictures. Duke's band became a magnet for the most talented musicians in this country. Chicago bassist Ernest Outlaw said: "There was no one like

EDWARD "DUKE" ELLINGTON WAS A COMMON MAN WHO ROSE TO ROYALTY. HIS LEGACY OF COMPOSING MORE THAN 1,000 UNIQUE SONGS SPANNING SEVERAL MUSICAL FORMS HAS EARNED HIM A PLACE IN HISTORY AS ONE OF AMERICA'S GREATEST COMPOSERS.

him. He always sought to do something different, something unique with his music. He blended sounds like no one else could. He was beyond category."

Historian Dempsey Travis agreed, "Duke's creative abilities reached into classical, gospel, and even African areas of music, in addition to the jazz that he popularized." Travis was interviewed on jazz station WNUA FM in Chicago, where he discussed his new book, *The Duke Ellington Primer.* "No other American composer had the depth and the production of Duke, which is why he is without question America's greatest composer."

Inspired by his fellow musicians and the high life he lived off the bandstand, Duke wrote more than 1,000 compositions. These include "It Don't Mean a Thing if It Ain't Got That Swing," "Satin Doll," "Sophisticated Lady," and his trademark tune written in collaboration with Billy Strayhorn, "Take the A Train."

Duke, as a person and as a composer, responded to the times. The Civil Rights Movement did not escape his perceptive eye. His contribution, while less vocal than others, was nevertheless very significant. In 1963, he wrote an ambitious show called, *My People.* He dedicated it to the immense contributions of many African Americans. The show received rave reviews when it played in Chicago that same year.

Two years later, the Pulitzer committee recommended that Ellington receive the famous prize, which is an honor given to the most accomplished individuals. The selection board made the unusual decision to ignore the committee's recommendation. Many felt racial bias was the motivation behind the

Facing page: *Duke's songs will live forever. His memorable classics include "Take the A Train" and "Satin Doll."* Left: *Despite not receiving the Pulitzer Prize for his music, Ellington would not become bitter. He eventually did receive recognition. President Richard Nixon gave him the Medal of Freedom Award, the highest award a civilian can receive.*

Above: *Duke with his best friend and collaborator, Billy Strayhorn (front). Strayhorn's death caused Ellington to release* And His Mother Called Him Bill, *a collection of all Strayhorn songs.*

Above: *Duke Ellington, his wife, and his band arrive in Hollywood in 1934. They were under contract to Paramount at the time and were scheduled to perform in a movie.* Facing page: *Duke readies his band to play one of his Sacred Concerts in a church.*

board's decision. Ellington was hurt that he didn't receive the Pulitzer. He mused, "Fate is being very kind to me. Fate doesn't want me to be too famous, too young." He was 66.

That same year, Ellington opened San Francisco's Grace Cathedral with the first of three sets of religious music that he called the Sacred Concerts. They consisted of both vocal and instrumental music composed for performance in large churches, synagogues, cathedrals, and mosques.

In 1967, Billy Strayhorn, friend and collaborator for almost three decades, died. The death of his best friend moved Ellington in ways few could predict. Later that year, he recorded *And His Mother Called Him Bill,* which featured all Strayhorn tunes. "Sweet Pea" Strayhorn's death inspired him in other ways, too.

Ellington composed, recorded, and toured at a hectic pace. In 1968, the National Academy of Recording Arts and Sciences finally honored him at age 69 with not one but two Grammy awards.

The Duke Ellington Orchestra continued to play their exciting brand of jazz, classical, African, spiritual, and ballet music. Ellington wrote the ballet *The River* for Alvin Ailey's dance company. Meanwhile, the group performed before Queen Elizabeth of England and the President of the United States, Richard Nixon, who gave Duke the Medal of Freedom Award, the highest honor a civilian can receive.

Duke Ellington, a chain smoker all his life, died of lung cancer in 1974. Yet, he lives on in the thousands of songs he left. Grammy Award–winning composer and musician Wynton Marsalis hails Duke Ellington as "America's greatest composer."

MEDGAR EVERS WAS THE MOST PROMINENT CIVIL RIGHTS LEADER IN THE STATE OF MISSISSIPPI BEFORE BEING ASSASSINATED JUNE 12, 1963 BY BYRON DE LA BECKWITH. THE MURDER INTENSIFIED THE CIVIL RIGHTS STRUGGLE AND WAS A FACTOR IN PRESIDENT JOHN KENNEDY ASKING CONGRESS TO ENACT MAJOR CIVIL RIGHTS LEGISLATION.

One of the most prominent Black leaders of the 1960s Civil Rights Movement in the state of Mississippi, Medgar Evers also became one of the Civil Rights Movement's most important martyrs.

Not that the death of any one human being during that turbulent struggle was worth more or less than others who were killed, but the first murder of a nationally known civil rights leader showed the world the degree to which racial violence was practiced in the South.

Evers's death led to increased participation in the movement by outraged Americans, which led to even more demonstrations and violence, and was a motivating factor in President John Kennedy's decision a week later to ask Congress to enact comprehensive civil rights legislation.

Medgar Evers was born July 2, 1925, in Decatur, Mississippi, to strongly religious parents—his father was a farmer and sawmill operator, his mother a domestic worker who took in ironing. Evers attended a one-room elementary school in Decatur, then later, he walked 12 miles to high school in nearby Newton.

After serving in Normandy during World War II, Evers returned home in 1946 and enrolled in Alcorn A&M College, where he was a popular student—a business administration major and school newspaper editor.

Evers met his wife, Myrlie, there; they had three children.

Following college, he sold life insurance, but left that to join the NAACP—and the growing Civil Rights Movement—in 1952. Evers became the group's Mississippi field secretary in 1954. After the Supreme Court outlawed public school segregation that year, he actively sought enforcement of the ruling in his state, which had one of the most rigid systems of segregation.

In 1962, Evers played a key role in enrolling James Meredith as the first Black student at the University of Mississippi, a major victory in the early stages of the Civil Rights Movement.

He went on to spearhead a number of economic boycotts in downtown Jackson,

Mississippi, of businesses that practiced segregation. He also helped form the "Jackson Movement," an umbrella of Black organizations that sponsored mass demonstrations throughout the segregated state. The group demanded integration of all public facilities and institutions and increased job opportunities for Blacks on city payrolls. But at the time, opposition to the Civil Rights Movement was perhaps at its most entrenched and violent, especially in Mississippi.

On June 12, 1963, as he returned home, Evers was shot in the back by Byron de la Beckwith, a fertilizer salesman and member of an old Mississippi family. It took three trials and 30 years before Beckwith was convicted.

Medgar Evers, 38, was buried in Arlington National Cemetery with full military honors.

Facing page: *Evers's strongest skill was his ability to negotiate with various groups.* Left: *Evers (facing the camera, right) and Roy Wilkins (facing the camera, left) are arrested in 1963, after trying to picket Woolworth's segregated lunch counter in Jackson, Mississippi.*

LOUIS FARRAKHAN

LOUIS FARRAKHAN

IS THE LEADER OF THE NATION OF
ISLAM AND A SPELLBINDING
ORATOR WHO PREACHES BLACK
SELF-RELIANCE, INDEPENDENCE,
AND ECONOMIC SELF-SUFFICIENCY.
FARRAKHAN, CONSIDERED A
RACIST BY SOME, INITIATED AND
CO-ORGANIZED THE HISTORIC
1995 MILLION MAN MARCH ON
WASHINGTON, D.C.

Louis Farrakhan is the Honorable Minister of the Nation of Islam, based in Chicago, with mosques in more than 120 cities. An intense speaker with a strong belief in Black independence, Farrakhan has been a thorn in the side of White America since converting to Islam in 1955. He tells his followers to buy Black, live clean, and take care of their own. But Farrakhan's penchant for making anti-Jewish remarks have made him a pariah in some quarters, and many consider him a racist.

African-American leaders are often asked to disavow Farrakhan. But Farrakhan says, "whenever any Black person...rises to speak against the norm that we have accepted as truth, it creates what you call controversy."

The eloquent, magnetic Farrakhan was born in the Bronx, New York, May 11, 1933, to parents who supported Black nationalist Marcus Garvey. Farrakhan attended Winston-Salem Teachers College in North Carolina. He married in 1953 and has nine children.

Farrakhan, an accomplished musician, was performing in Chicago in 1955 when he first heard Nation of Islam leader Elijah Muhammad speak. After sampling the fiery oratory of Malcolm X, Farrakhan joined the Nation that same year. He ran the Boston temple, then took over in Harlem after Malcolm X was murdered. There have been questions as to whether Farrakhan was involved in the assassination, which he vehemently denies.

In 1975, Farrakhan took over the Nation's leadership. He has worked to restore many of the Nation's businesses, he reopened the Chicago mosque, and he opened a school that taught Muslim traditions.

But Farrakhan's speeches exhorting Blacks to defend themselves against White racism and economic repression, stressing the importance of the Black male and family structure, and raging against Whites (especially Jews) for their crimes against African Americans, have made him a controversial figure. He says he wants Jews to "let my people go,"

Facing page: *In 1993, Farrakhan speaks at a rally to stop Black on Black violence.* Right: *Farrakhan speaks at the Million Man March in Washington, D.C. on October 16, 1995. This was the largest assembly of African Americans since the 1963 March on Washington. Farrakhan's son Mustafa is standing to the left of him.*

and to stop threatening to cut off funds to Black groups who "take a path not desired by outsiders."

Farrakhan initiated and co-organized the Million Man March on Washington, D.C., in October 1995, with the Rev. Benjamin Chavis, Jr. Black men were asked to atone for the mistakes of the past.

In 1996, he took his message of reconciliation to 23 Arab and African countries, including Libya and Nigeria, saying money and support from the nations would help him revitalize Black urban communities. The U.S. government has threatened an investigation, saying he may have compromised national security. Farrakhan, calling himself an "agent of God," says he was trying to link the interests of Blacks and Muslims worldwide. He continues to lead the Nation of Islam. He currently lives in Chicago.

T. THOMAS FORTUNE

WAS A JOURNALIST AND CIVIL RIGHTS LEADER WHO USED HIS CLARION VOICE TO WAGE WAR ON DISCRIMINATION AND RACIAL REPRESSION. FORTUNE FOUNDED THE NEW YORK AGE, A MILITANT PUBLICATION THAT DEMANDED FULL EQUALITY FOR BLACKS.

Timothy Thomas Fortune spent his life fighting to free African Americans from racial discrimination. He also worked to keep infighting among Blacks from costing them hard-won gains, politically and economically. Editor and founder of several African-American newspapers, Fortune attempted to convince Black power brokers to consolidate their forces to achieve true equality for the race.

Fortune was born to slave parents in Marianna, Florida, in October of 1856, with the blood of Blacks, Native Americans, and Irish Whites flowing through his veins. His family's political activities forced them to flee to Jacksonville, Florida, where Fortune had a limited education through the Freedmen's Bureau. Fortune learned the printer's trade and became an expert at composition.

He briefly attended Howard University in Washington, D.C., in 1876, and began his love affair with journalism while working on the *People's Advocate.* While working for this Black newspaper, Fortune met and married

Carrie C. Smiley. They later returned to his native Florida.

In the late 1870s, Fortune moved to New York, first as a printer, then almost immediately as part-owner of the weekly tabloid *Rumor.* Fortune became editor of the newspaper, changing its name to the *Globe.* The trailblazing writer then became sole owner of his first newspaper, *The New York Freeman,* which later became *New York Age.* He believed the paper's purpose was to counter negative coverage of Blacks by the White press.

"The great newspapers, which should plead the cause of the oppressed and the downtrodden, which should be the palladiums of the people's rights, are all on the side of the oppressor, or by silence preserve a dignified but ignominious neutrality," wrote Fortune. "Day after day they weave a false picture of facts—facts which must measurably influence the future historian of the times in the composition of impartial history. The wrongs of the masses are referred to sneeringly or apologetically."

Fortune's editorial policies advocated Black self-reliance, demanded full equality for African Americans, and condemned all forms of discrimination. In an 1883 editorial, Fortune blasted the U.S. Supreme Court for its decisions in several cases, noting that "We are declared to be created equal, and entitled to certain rights, . . . but there is no law to protect us in the enjoyment of them."

Two general circulation papers, the *Boston Transcript* and the *New York Sun,* hired Fortune as a reporter and editor, which was unusual for a Black man in the 1880s. Fortune traveled the South, reporting on the conditions. Fortune was an early advocate of the term Afro-American. He considered Negro to be a term of contempt.

Fortune also wrote three books. *Black and White: Land and Politics in the South* (1884), a historical essay on land, labor, and politics in the South, called for the unification of workers of both races. He also wrote *The Negro in Politics,* which was published in 1885, and then *Dreams of Life,* published in 1905.

Fortune later founded the National Afro-American League, an organization that pioneered many programs and methods used by many modern-day civil rights groups. He told the delegates at the Chicago event that "before the rights conferred upon us by the war amendments are fully conceded, a full century will have passed away. We have undertaken no child's play. We have undertaken a serious work which will tax and exhaust the best intelligence and energy of the race for the next century."

The League was short-lived. However, in 1898, Fortune's National Afro-American Council held a conference emphasizing civil rights, women's suffrage, and concern over the fate of Latin Americans after the United States defeated Spain. Political infighting over Fortune's support of Black leader Booker T. Washington severely weakened the organization. The legacies of Fortune's groups helped set the platform for the NAACP, formally organized in 1910, and that group's ongoing fight for an end to discrimination in all forms.

Fortune suffered a bout of mental illness in the early 1900s, possibly related to alcoholism. He was virtually a derelict for several years. When his health returned, Fortune returned to writing fiery editorials for Black nationalist Marcus Garvey's *Negro World.*

Fortune died in Philadelphia in 1928. Kelly Miller of Howard University eulogized him as "the best developed journalist that the Negro race has produced in the Western World."

Facing page and above: *Fortune's* New York Age *was his forum for countering negative press from White papers and demanding full equality for African Americans. He also worked to convince other Black leaders to consolidate their power rather than fighting among themselves.*

JOHN HOPE FRANKLIN

JOHN HOPE FRANKLIN,

HISTORIAN, EDUCATOR, AND

PROLIFIC AUTHOR, HAS SPENT HIS

LIFE TEACHING PEOPLE ABOUT THE

CONTRIBUTIONS AFRICAN

AMERICANS HAVE MADE TO

HISTORY. FRANKLIN'S LEGACY

MAKES IT POSSIBLE FOR BLACKS TO

UNDERSTAND THEIR IMPORTANCE

IN BUILDING AND MAINTAINING

THE AMERICAN DREAM.

John Hope Franklin is living proof that African Americans play an invaluable role in interpreting the importance of Blacks in history. Franklin, who has been awarded more than 30 honorary degrees and has been a professor at many universities, uses his vast knowledge and clarion voice to trumpet the accomplishments of Blacks in helping to build this country.

Franklin was born January 2, 1915, in Rentiesville, Ohio, the son of Mollie and Buck Franklin. An advocate of education, Franklin graduated magna cum laude from Fisk University in Nashville, a legendary haven for scores of America's best and brightest Blacks. Franklin then enrolled in Harvard University, receiving his master's degree in 1936. The dark-skinned, slim man returned to Fisk to teach for a year, but went back to Harvard for his Ph.D. in 1941.

Believing that education is a path to freedom and equality for Blacks, Franklin launched a journey that included passing his knowledge to students at several colleges and universities. In North Carolina, Franklin taught at St. Augustine's College while writing a dissertation on free Blacks in that state. He moved on to North Carolina College in Durham, North Carolina, in 1943, then to Howard University in Washington, D.C., four years later. In the meantime, Franklin earned prestigious Rosenwald and Guggenheim fellowships for research.

Brooklyn College invited the brilliant young scholar to join its faculty in 1956. Eight years later, Franklin became a professor of history at the University of Chicago, the first major White university to tenure an African-American scholar. Franklin chaired the history department there, and was named the first John Matthews Manly Distinguished Service Professor of History. In 1982, Franklin held the post of James B. Duke Professor of History at Duke University in North Carolina. He retired from that position in 1985 and accepted the appointment as professor of legal history at Duke University Law School. He currently teaches constitutional law at Duke University.

Franklin's achievements haven't been limited to teaching. In 1949, he was the first Black to read a paper before the prestigious Southern Historical Association, and later became its president. Franklin was also the first African-American president of the American Historical Association, Phi Beta Kappa, and the Organization of American Historians. He was one of the social scientists who drew up the historical brief for the NAACP's legal argument for the plaintiff's cause in the historic *Brown* v. *Board of Education* case.

A prolific author, Franklin's many books include *The Free Negro in North Carolina, 1790–1860* (1943); *From Slavery to Freedom* (1947, seventh edition 1994), an outstanding college reference and textbook; and *A Southern Odyssey: Travelers in the Antebellum North* (1976). He also wrote the award-winning *George Washington Williams: A Biography,* which was published in 1985. Franklin's other honors are too numerous to list, including other professional offices, fellowships, and honorary doctorates.

A lifelong champion of civil rights, Franklin spoke against Judge Robert Bork's confirmation as a U.S. Supreme Court Justice before a Senate committee in 1987. Franklin is married and has one son.

Franklin helped produce the historic brief for the NAACP's legal team that argued and won the Brown v. Board of Education *Supreme Court case in 1954. That decision ended segregation in public schools. In the 1960s, Franklin became the first tenured African-American scholar at a major White university when he became a history professor at the University of Chicago.*

MARCUS GARVEY

Marcus Garvey not only rocked the boat, but opted to transport Blacks back to Africa by boat. This message would be both his calling card and his swan song.

Marcus Moziah Garvey was born in 1887, in St. Anns Bay, Jamaica. His father, Marcus, was a stonemason by trade and a descendant of the Maroon tribesmen, who 200 years earlier had organized slave revolts and created autonomous societies.

By age 20, Garvey led a printer's strike. He was fired, earning a reputation as a social worker, a preacher for the poor, and a speaker for the dispossessed and working classes.

In 1910, Garvey left Jamaica for Costa Rica, where an uncle got him a job on a sugarcane plantation. That didn't last. He settled in an area where West Indians lived and started a newspaper, *La Nacion/The Nation,* which organized immigrants. After harassment from local authorities, he packed and traveled to other Latin American nations. Two years later, he visited Europe and worked on the docks of England. Then he traveled to France, Germany, Italy, and Austria, writing in many newspapers.

But it was not until 1914, when he returned to Jamaica, that Garvey's role in history would materialize. That is when he founded, on Jamaican Independence Day, the Universal Negro Improvement Association (UNIA). It soon became one of the largest independent Black mass organization the world had ever seen. Its simple message of race pride and self-reliance hit a chord among Blacks worldwide. UNIA was modeled after Booker T. Washington's Tuskegee Institute.

Inspired by Washington's *Up From Slavery,* Garvey left Jamaica in 1916 for the United States. He began a lecture tour that would organize chapters of the UNIA in America. In 1918, he started the *Negro World,* a newspaper that first published many major writers of the Harlem Renaissance and reached at least 50,000 readers.

Garvey was very successful, acquiring a bevy of businesses, including grocery stores, laundries, restaurants, hotels, and his prized Black Star Line—the steamship company he acquired in 1919 to link people of African descent all over the world. He ultimately bought three ships, naming them after Black leaders such as the "Booker T. Washington."

In 1920, he campaigned for $2 million and collected $137,000 in the first few months to organize the first International Convention of the UNIA. It attracted tens of thousands of followers who marched through Harlem in colorful uniforms honoring their famous soon-to-be-notorious philosopher-prophet. He sold stock to his followers and admirers under an arrangement that barred White purchasers, according to historian Lerone Bennett, Jr. Garvey created the red, black, and green UNIA flag, which would later represent Black liberation in this century. During this same period, he unsuccessfully appealed to the League of Nations, the precursor to the United Nations, to turn over German-held African nations to independent Black rule.

Garvey had enemies, the most famous of whom was W.E.B. Du Bois. Du Bois, cofounder of the NAACP, was an integrationist opposed to a Black separate state and the repatriation efforts of Garvey. Du Bois was also critical of Garvey's public association with the Klu Klux Klan, his criticism of "mulatto" Black leadership, and his belief in Black racial purity.

In 1923, when his steamship company went bankrupt, Garvey was convicted of mail fraud. He went to jail in 1925 for two years. His sentence was commuted by President Coolidge before he was deported to Jamaica. Garvey died in London of a stroke at age 53 without ever setting foot in Africa.

Garvey, shown in 1922, wearing his uniform as President of the Republic of Africa. Garvey was perhaps the foremost proponent of the "Back to Africa" movement popular among many African Americans in the early part of the 20th century. His desire to create separate Black states led Garvey to petition the League of Nations to turn over German-controlled African nations to Black rule following World War I.

A RESTLESS, TROUBLED YOUTH, ALTHEA GIBSON FOUND SOLACE, SUCCESS, AND HERSELF IN TENNIS. SHE BECAME THE FIRST BLACK PLAYER TO COMPETE AND WIN AT BOTH FOREST HILLS (U.S. OPEN) AND WIMBLEDON—A FEAT SHE ACCOMPLISHED IN 1957 AND REPEATED IN 1958.

Althea Gibson's life has been one of struggle, perseverance, and redemption. Overcoming an early pattern of erratic behavior, inconsistency, and being easily frustrated, she became the first Black player to win tennis championships at Wimbledon and the U.S. Open.

Gibson was born August 25, 1927, in Silver, South Carolina. She and her sharecropper parents relocated to Harlem while she was still a child. In New York, the pretty, gangly girl was frequently truant in school—prone to playing hooky and spending days at the movies.

Eventually placed in a foster home, Gibson was an embittered, restless malcontent who couldn't hold a job. But she showed remarkable prowess in street basketball, stickball, and table tennis. A New York City recreation department worker noticed her talents and introduced her to his friend Fred Johnson, a tennis pro at Harlem's elite Cosmopolitan Club.

Shortly after Gibson won her first tournament, the New York Open Championship in 1942, Cosmopolitan Club members pooled their resources to send her to more tournaments, where she did well. Gibson caught the eye of two Black doctors who were leaders in the American Tennis Association and they became her sponsors. Beginning in 1947, she won the first of ten ATA National Championships.

Her tennis success made Gibson a better student. In 1949, she graduated from high school ranked 10th in her class and went on to Florida A&M College.

Gibson's tennis ability was not to be denied. She received invitations to play in eastern and national indoor championships and then, in 1950, became the first Black woman asked to play in the U.S. National Championship Tournament at Forest Hills, now known as the U.S. Open.

Though eliminated in the second round, Gibson traveled to Europe, Mexico, and Southeast Asia, winning 16 of 18 tournaments. That secured her a bid to Wimbledon.

But Gibson was defeated in that tournament and then again that year at Forest Hills. It wasn't until 1957 that she won the U.S. National and her first Wimbledon title. In 1958, she won both tournaments again.

Then, surprisingly, at the age of 30, Gibson gave up tennis to pursue other activities and make the money that tennis, at that point, didn't provide. She recorded albums, acted briefly, toured with the Harlem Globetrotters, and became a celebrity endorser.

Gibson played pro golf from 1963 to 1967 as the first Black member of the Ladies Professional Golf Association. Later she worked for the New Jersey State Athletic Control Board and has served as special consultant to the New Jersey Governor's Council on Physical Fitness and Sports since 1988.

Left: *Gibson plays Shirley Bloomer in 1958, in the Wightman Cup in Wimbledon. Gibson was the reigning Wimbledon champion at the time.* Right: *Gibson in 1950, while waiting for an invitation to play in the National Tennis Tournament at Forest Hills. She was the first African-American player invited to the tournament.*

BERRY GORDY, JR.

Berry Gordy, Jr., parlayed a spare time hobby of writing songs into the most successful African-American owned record company in history, and changed the sound of pop music along the way.

His Motown Records, started in 1959, became the world's largest independent record company, the first major Black-owned company in the entertainment industry, and America's largest Black business in 1973, with sales of more than $50 million.

Through Motown, which became a virtual music factory and produced hits as though they came off the assembly line, Gordy engineered super-stardom for such talents as Stevie Wonder, Michael Jackson, Diana Ross, Marvin Gaye, Smokey Robinson, The Temptations, and Martha and the Vandellas.

Born November 28, 1929, in Detroit, one of eight children, Gordy dropped out of high school in the 11th grade to pursue a boxing career. That path ended when he was drafted into the army, where he earned his high school equivalency diploma while serving in Korea from 1951 to 1953.

Back in Detroit after the war, Gordy worked at the Ford Motor Company while writing songs when he had the chance. His break-through came when a young singer named Jackie Wilson recorded Gordy's song "Reet Petite," which became Wilson's first hit in 1957. In the next two years, Gordy wrote four more hits for Wilson, including "Lonely Teardrops" in 1958.

By then, Gordy had befriended another young singer named Smokey Robinson, who talked him into opening his own recording studio. With the aid of an $800 loan from his family, Berry opened his company.

The hits began immedi-ately. The "Motown Sound" consisted of sophisticated rhythm-and-blues augmented by slick symphonic orchestra-tions. It not only appealed to African Americans, but crossed over to White America as well.

Motown's first number one pop hit came that year with "Please Mr. Postman." In 1962, when the company had 11 R&B top 10 hits, it had four singles in the pop top 10. The next year it had six, with Stevie Wonder's "Finger-

tips, Part 2" reaching number one. In 1964, five Motown hits were number one on the pop charts. The legend of Motown was born.

In 1972, Gordy moved the company to Los Angeles and branched off into films, making the successful *Lady Sings the Blues,* for which star Diana Ross received an Academy Award nomination, and *The Bingo Long Traveling All-Stars and Motor Kings*. Gordy's TV special *Motown 25—Yesterday, Today, and Forever,* in 1983, was the most watched variety special in television history, and 1985's *Motown Returns to the Apollo* won an Emmy award.

Gordy sold Motown Records to MCA Inc. in 1984 for $61 million, but retained Motown's publishing company Jobete Music.

Left: *A young Gordy, at the beginning of his Motown career.* Right: *Gordy's contributions to the music industry are legendary. In 1988, he was acknowledged with his induction into the Rock and Roll Hall of Fame.*

FANNIE LOU HAMER

A TIRELESS DRUM MAJOR FOR AFRICAN-AMERICAN POLITICAL EMPOWERMENT, FANNIE LOU HAMER WAS A BRIGHT LIGHT IN THE FIRMAMENT OF THE 1960S CIVIL RIGHTS STRUGGLE. "SICK AND TIRED OF BEING SICK AND TIRED," HAMER SPENT HER LIFE FIGHTING FOR EQUALITY.

Fannie Lou Hamer was a farmer and educator who became a beacon of hope for the nation's poor and politically disenfranchised. Born in the rural South, Hamer became a powerful voice in the fight for Black equality and self-reliance. Hamer's actions helped change some of the National Democratic Party's racist policies, and she increased Black political power by registering voters in the South.

Hamer has said one of the things that made her so committed to helping poor people was watching her sharecropping parents struggle to raise their 20 children in rural Mississippi. She was born there, in Montgomery County, October 6, 1917, and was working in the cotton fields by the time she was six years old. When she was 13, Hamer could pick 300 to 400 pounds of cotton per day and was troubled by the economic disparity between the Black workers and the White plantation owners. She married Perry Hamer in 1942, and for 18 years she worked as a sharecropper.

But in 1962, Hamer burst upon the civil rights scene after attending a stirring rally for the Southern Christian Leadership Conference (SCLC) and the Student Nonviolent Coordinating Committee (SNCC). She volunteered to challenge voting laws, but had to

Hamer and others protested the regular Mississippi Democratic Party's all-White delegation at the 1964 Democratic Presidential Convention in Atlantic City.

flee her plantation for trying to register to vote. Hamer was threatened and survived a gun attack. In 1963, she passed the literacy test many Southern states used to keep Blacks from voting, and she registered.

Hamer's commitment to the movement caught fire. She became a field-worker for the SNCC. Hamer believed there was a link between Black lack of access to the political process and widespread Black poverty. She helped start Delta Ministry, a community development program. Hamer continued to register voters, and as a result was injured in a brutal beating at a rural Mississippi jail.

Since the state's Democratic party wouldn't allow Black participation, Hamer helped found the Mississippi Freedom Democratic Party (MFDP) in 1964. That group made national headlines by challenging the seating of the all-White Mississippi delegation to the Democratic National Convention in Atlantic City. Hamer spoke to the group in a televised hearing, telling the nation about the plight of Blacks trying to exercise their right to vote. She was a delegate to the 1968 convention.

Later, Hamer founded the Freedom Farms Cooperation, which helped needy families get food and livestock. She worked with day-care centers and developers building homes for the poor and spoke nationwide on behalf of Black self-reliance. Hamer spoke for many oppressed African Americans when she told America, "I'm sick and tired of being sick and tired."

A lifelong force of strength for her people, Hamer died of cancer March 14, 1977.

Below: *After the U.S. House of Representatives rejected a challenge to the election of five Mississippi representatives in 1964, Hamer spoke to sympathizers outside the Capitol in Washington, D.C. Noting that Blacks were excluded from the election process in Mississippi, Hamer declared, "We'll come back year after year until we are allowed our rights as citizens."*

William Christopher Handy's father was a former slave and Methodist minister who discouraged his son's interest in music but allowed him to pursue it only if he didn't get involved in what his parents called "that low-down" music—ragtime and blues. But Handy was a teenager; he wanted to do what teens of any era want to do—swing with the rhythms of the day.

Handy was born November 16, 1873, in Florence, Alabama. In high school, he studied organ and trained in formal music theory to satisfy his parents, but on the side he played cornet in a local brass band and sang with church groups and minstrel troupes.

By age 18, he was an outstanding trumpet player. Two years later, his quartet enjoyed acclaim after appearing at the Chicago Columbian Exposition of 1893. Buoyed by that success, Handy's band toured the United States, Mexico, and Cuba, playing ragtime and minstrel music, including the marches of John Philip Sousa and the songs of Stephen Foster.

Traveling through the South, Handy became enamored of the rich musical heritage perpetuated by Black itinerant blues singers playing on homemade guitars.

In Memphis in 1909, a political jingle he wrote in a bluesy fashion for a mayoral candidate (the infamous "Boss" Crump) enjoyed widespread popularity. Stimulated by that success, Handy started composing blues songs and collecting Black folk music, which he published in blues form. This folk music was dramatically different from traditional Black spirituals and work songs. The most famous of these pieces is "St. Louis Blues," which Handy had published in 1914.

He moved to New York to make his first recordings in 1918. Soon, his highly successful publishing company led the field in introducing the music of African-American songwriters to the general public. This led to the "race records" marketing craze of the 1920s. Handy's songs became national hits and moneymakers.

Because of his formal training, Handy was able to capture in written form what was basically orally handed-down folk music of Blacks in the South. His success in the commercial marketplace then allowed him to promote this music nationally and eventually worldwide. If not for Handy, the blues may have remained virtually unknown or stayed in regional obscurity.

Handy lost his sight following World War I, then partially regained it. Then, in 1943, he fell from a subway platform and became totally blind. He suffered a stroke in 1955, which left him wheelchair-bound, and died March 28, 1958, from pneumonia.

Handy was survived by his second wife, Louise, whom he had married at the age of 80, the same year that Handy was portrayed in the movie *St. Louis Blues* by Nat "King" Cole.

Left: *Handy stands in front of a poster of one of his many popular songs.* Right: *Handy in 1949. Despite being blind, he still appeared frequently at benefits and concerts.*

LORRAINE HANSBERRY

A bright star who blazed brilliantly but whose light died out too soon, Lorraine Hansberry wrote the play that is credited with giving birth to the modern Black American theater.

A Raisin in the Sun opened on Broadway in 1959. It won the distinguished New York Drama Critics Circle Award that year over such heavy competition as plays by Tennessee Williams, Eugene O'Neill, and Archibald MacLeish.

Her brilliant work, about the experiences and aspirations of a poor Black family living in a Chicago ghetto, was Hansberry's first play. She began writing it at the age of 26, and when she received the Drama Critics Circle Award at age 29, she was the youngest playwright, the fifth woman, and the first Black to receive the honor.

The Broadway production, which ran for 19 months, starred such notable actors as Sidney Poitier, Diana Sands, Claudia McNeil, and Ruby Dee. This original cast also starred in the movie version of the work, which won the Best Picture Award, along with other awards, at the Cannes Film Festival in 1961.

Unfortunately, *A Raisin in the Sun* was the height of Hansberry's short career—she died of cancer six years after its debut on January 12, 1965, at the age of 34.

Hansberry was born May 19, 1930, in Chicago to a well-to-do family. Her parents opened a successful real estate firm and one of the first Black banks in Chicago. The home of her youth was frequented by such luminaries as Walter White, Jesse Owens, Langston Hughes, Duke Ellington, and Paul Robeson.

Hansberry studied art, English, and stage design for two years at the University of Wisconsin, then moved to New York in 1950. There she joined Paul Robeson's Harlem-based *Freedom* magazine. As associate editor from 1952 to 1953, she wrote articles dealing with Africa, women's issues, and social issues. She also wrote several reviews of plays, which provided the impetus for her to write her own plays.

After *A Raisin in the Sun*, Hansberry worked on a number of projects, most of which remained uncompleted, including a novel and collection of essays. Her last completed stage work was *The Sign in Sidney Brustein's Window*, about a Greenwich Village intellectual and his role in a local election. The play made it to Broadway in 1964 for 101 performances and was still running when Hansberry died.

After her death, her unpublished papers were assembled into the play *To Be Young, Gifted and Black*, which toured nationally from 1970 to 1971 and was later expanded into Hansberry's biography.

Left: *Hansberry was the first African-American woman to have a play presented on Broadway. The title of the work,* A Raisin in the Sun, *came from a line from Langston Hughes's poem "Harlem," which noted that a dream deferred would dry up, "like a raisin in the sun."* Right: *Actors Ruby Dee, Sidney Poitier, and Diana Sands starred in both the triumphant Broadway and screen versions of Hansberry's masterpiece.*

DOROTHY IRENE HEIGHT

SOCIAL ACTIVIST

DOROTHY HEIGHT HAS SPENT DECADES TRUMPETING THE FIGHT FOR AFRICAN-AMERICAN CIVIL RIGHTS, WOMEN'S ISSUES, AND ECONOMIC WELL-BEING FOR PEOPLE WORLDWIDE. HEIGHT'S WORK WITH MANY PRIVATE AND GOVERNMENT SOCIAL SERVICE AGENCIES HAS HELPED MILLIONS.

Dorothy Irene Height is a social worker focused on improving conditions for Blacks, women, and the poor. Her clarion oratory, plus her work with groups ranging from the Young Women's Christian Association (YWCA), Delta Sigma Theta Sorority, Inc. (DST), and the National Council of Negro Women (NCNW) have made her a leader in the battle for equality and human rights. Height's current project centers on revitalizing African-American family values.

Height was born March 24, 1912, in Richmond, Virginia. Her family moved to the small mining town of Rankin, Pennsylvania, where Height was a tall, straight-A student who excelled in athletics. She was active in the YWCA as a teenager, and has stayed involved most of her life. Height went to New York University for college, earning both her bachelor's and master's degrees in four years. She also studied at Columbia University and the New York School of Social Work.

Height's youth club activities took her to several Christian youth conferences in the United States, Holland, and England. She also helped Eleanor Roosevelt plan a 1938 World Youth Congress in New York. At the same time, Height worked for New York's Welfare Department, and was asked to examine the unrest following the 1935 riots in Harlem. During this period, Height met NCNW founder and magnetic civil rights activist Mary McLeod Bethune. Height began volunteering in the group's quest for women's rights.

Height began her long career with the YWCA in 1938, running a lodging home for Black women in Harlem, then later in Washington, D.C. The powerful speaker ran training programs for YWCA volunteers and developed programs for interracial education. Height eventually helped desegregate the YWCA and later directed its Center for Racial Justice.

In 1939, Height began her tenure with DST, guiding the national Black sorority toward a greater commitment to activism. She was national president from 1947 to 1956, during which time she established the group's first international chapter in Haiti, and she organized bookmobiles for African-American communities in the South.

Height then took on one of her most powerful positions, as president of NCNW, an umbrella group for women's rights organizations. The council's goals include uniting Black women of all classes and stressing interrace cooperation. During Height's tenure, NCNW has helped women open businesses, sponsored job training, and run voter

registration programs. Height continues to guide its fight for equal rights for women of color worldwide. Since 1986, the council has sponsored annual celebrations nationwide called Black Family Reunions. These reunions are an attempt to renew the concept of the ex-

tended Black family and thereby to improve social conditions.

Height, the recipient of numerous awards and honorary degrees, continues to be a firebrand in the struggle to improve the lives of Blacks and women.

During the 1990 visit of South African Ambassador Dr. Pete Koornhof (left) to the United States, as pressure escalated on his country to end apartheid, Height and Jesse Jackson joined him in singing "We Shall Overcome."

CHARLES HOUSTON

CHARLES HOUSTON

WAS THE LEGAL ARCHITECT

RETAINED BY THE NAACP AS

SPECIAL COUNSEL TO HELP

DISMANTLE DISCRIMINATION IN

PUBLIC EDUCATION AND

TRANSPORTATION. HIS SUCCESSFUL

ARGUMENTS BEFORE THE SUPREME

COURT AND OTHER BODIES SET

THE GROUNDWORK FOR THE

BROWN V. BOARD OF EDUCATION

CASE THAT EVENTUALLY ENDED ALL

LEGALLY SANCTIONED

SEGREGATION IN AMERICA.

Charles Hamilton Houston was a brilliant lawyer. His successful appearances before the U.S. Supreme Court on matters of racial discrimination laid the groundwork for the landmark *Brown* v. *Topeka, Kansas Board of Education* case. This case ended racial segregation in public schools. Because the *Brown* case led to further court decisions outlawing various other forms of discrimination and to legislation enacting civil rights laws, it can be said that Houston had a major impact on dismantling legally sanctioned racism in America.

Born September 3, 1895, in Washington, D.C., Houston showed his brilliance early when he graduated from high school at the age of 15. He then graduated from Amherst College four years later as a Phi Beta Kappa and one of six class valedictorians.

Houston earned his law degree from Harvard University in 1922, graduating cum laude and in the top five percent of his class. He became the first Black student selected as an editor of the *Harvard Law Review* and, in 1923, the first African American awarded a doctor of judicial science degree from Harvard.

That same year, he received a one-year fellowship to study civil law at the University of Madrid. Houston was admitted to the D.C. bar in 1924. From 1924 to 1950, Houston had a private practice with his father, William, who was a graduate of Howard University's law school. During those years, however, there were various interruptions in Houston's practice.

Houston also taught at Howard. As vice dean, appointed in 1929, he was in charge of the university's three-year day program and the law school library. His most notable accomplishments there were helping the law school receive accreditation from legal sanctioning bodies and significantly improving the curriculum.

In 1934, Houston took a leave of absence from Howard. The NAACP retained him as special counsel to direct a campaign against discrimination in public education and transportation. This work would establish the strategy of the NAACP to end all legal segregation. His assistant special counsel was Thurgood Marshall, who would go on successfully to argue the *Brown* case in 1954.

In two of Houston's early Supreme Court cases, in 1935 and 1938, the court overturned death sentences of Black defendants who had been convicted by juries from which Blacks had been excluded because of race. In 1938, Houston also won his argument in *Missouri ex rel. Gaines* v. *Canada*. The Supreme Court ruled that the state of Missouri could not bar Blacks from entering the state university law school without providing a separate but equal law school for Blacks.

The *Missouri* case was a major victory for Houston and for the NAACP. It forced the Supreme Court to take a hard look at the good-faith efforts of states to provide equal accommodations under the "separate but equal" policy. In this case, Missouri had been willing to provide scholarships for African Americans willing to go to other states to study law. However, the Supreme Court saw that as a way for Missouri to duck the expense of maintaining its own state law school for Black students.

In the 1940s, as a member of the NAACP's National Legal Committee and as general counsel of the Association of Colored Railway Trainmen and Locomotive Firemen and of the International Association of Railroad Employees, Houston argued two successful cases before the Court that outlawed racial discrimination in union bargaining representation.

When Houston passed away in April 1950, from a heart ailment at the age of 55, five Supreme Court justices attended his funeral. He was respected in legal circles for his ability as a constitutional lawyer and for the brilliance of his attacks on discrimination.

This brilliant legal strategist was one of the most gifted constitutional lawyers the Black community, or any community, has ever produced. Working primarily on behalf of the NAACP, Houston's victories before the Supreme Court helped end legal discrimination in America.

LANGSTON HUGHES

*WAS A POET WITH THE GENIUS TO
SET HIS MELLIFLUOUS VOICE TO
MUSIC—BOTH LITERALLY AND
FIGURATIVELY. A PROLIFIC
NOVELIST AND PLAYWRIGHT AS
WELL, HUGHES USED VERSE TO
ILLUSTRATE BLACK URBAN LIFE
AND ATTACK SOCIAL INJUSTICE.*

Langston Hughes wrote poetry from the time he was a child. His devastatingly observant yet sorrowful examinations of African-American life in Harlem, and the Black experience in general, are considered to be some of the most powerful writings of the 20th century. One of Hughes's most famous poems, "I, Too, Sing America," is a powerful plea to the country to recognize and accept Blacks on the basis of their myriad contributions. He was mentor to a generation of writers. Hughes was one of the most important voices of the Harlem Renaissance of the 1920s, and of the Civil Rights Movement of the 1960s.

> Happiness lives nowhere,
> Some old folk said,
> If not within oneself.

That line, from Hughes's poem "I Thought It Was Tangiers I Wanted," speaks volumes about the life of a man whose travels took him to some of the world's most exotic places, including Mexico, Spain, and Africa. Born in February of 1902, Hughes had already lived in seven cities in the U.S. and Mexico by the time he was 12. The handsome writer had been class poet in grammar school, and he didn't lay down his pen throughout his life. For several years after school he traveled, teaching and working as a servant. Then in 1924, writer and critic Vachel Lindsay "discovered" Hughes. He dubbed him the "bus boy poet."

In 1926, Hughes published his first book of poetry, *The Weary Blues,* followed by several volumes remarkable for the musical nature of the language. In later works, Hughes sometimes gave directions for musical accompaniment to his verses, making him one of the earliest writers to combine the two forms. One of Hughes's plays, *Mulatto* (1935), had a successful run on Broadway in New York. In the 1940s, Hughes created Jesse B. Simple, a fictional character in Hughes's *Chicago Defender* column, who represented the lives and racial consciousness of the Black working class.

In all, Hughes published more than ten volumes of poetry, a little over 60 dramas, and

scores of operas, anthologies of other Black writers, and two autobiographies. During the 1930s, Hughes took aim at civil rights and economic issues. Ten years later, Hughes took his genius for observation and his talent for relating to the working class to several universities. He taught at Atlanta University, then he was poet-in-residence at the University of Chicago's Laboratory School. In the 1960s, Hughes turned out an incredible volume of material, including *Ask Your Mama: 12 Moods for Jazz* (1961), and his last volume of poetry, *The Panther and the Lash* (1967).

Hughes, considered by many to be the "poet laureate of Harlem," died of congestive heart failure in New York in March 1967.

Facing page: The young Hughes was nicknamed the "bus boy poet" by critic Vachel Lindsay. Above: Hughes appeared before a Senate committee investigating communism in 1953. He said that he had been sympathetic to the Soviet form of government, but had never joined the Communist party.

ZORA NEALE HURSTON

WAS A MAJOR CONTRIBUTOR TO THE HARLEM RENAISSANCE. SHE WAS ALSO AN ANTHROPOLOGIST, PLAYWRIGHT, NOVELIST, AND FEMINIST WHO NEVER ACHIEVED TRUE FAME IN HER LIFETIME BECAUSE SHE WAS AN OUTSPOKEN, PROUD, BLACK WOMAN.

Critics and readers alike marvel at the woman we've come to know as Zora Neale Hurston. A writer, anthropologist, and eccentric personality who reigned during the 1920s and 1930s, Hurston created a stir just about every time she appeared in public.

Always outspoken, flamboyant, and colorful, Hurston never backed down from anyone—friend or foe. She spoke her mind and she wrote with the same ferocious clarity. In doing so, she created a legion of fans who have spanned generations. But during her own lifetime, Hurston stepped on many toes, and those people exacted sweet revenge on her. She proudly said that being misunderstood was the price she paid for daring to be great. And great she was.

Hurston created a prolific body of writings—plays, essays, novels, short stories, and anthropological studies—that both titillated and taunted the working and upper classes of Blacks and Whites. Her sterling masterpiece, *Their Eyes Were Watching God,* thrust her into literary dominance as a major player of the Harlem Renaissance. Ironically, after a few decades of being a celebrity, she died unnoticed in Florida from a long illness and was buried in a pauper's grave.

Hurston was born January 7, 1891, in the all-Black town of Eatonville, Florida. She lived a joyful young life. Her parents and her neighbors gave her the kind of support that was not always available to African Americans groping with survival under racial discrimination and a lack of economic opportunities. The world she knew broke apart, however, when her mother died in 1904. Her father then sent her to a boarding school, and her family scattered.

Hurston wandered from job to job until she found a position as a maid and wardrobe assistant in a traveling Gilbert and Sullivan theater company. During this period, she was bitten by the showbiz bug, but she finished high school at Morgan Academy in Baltimore. She received her college education at Howard University, and then earned a graduate degree in anthropology from Barnard College, where she studied under Franz Boas.

With the help of literary lions Charles S. Johnson and Alain Locke, she began her illustrious career by publishing short stories in *Opportunity* magazine. Collaborating with

Langston Hughes and Wallace Thurman, Hurston edited *Fire!* magazine.

Four years later, Hurston cowrote *Mule Bone* with Hughes. It is a comedy about African-American life that was never performed during her lifetime because Hurston and Hughes later had a falling out over personal and professional reasons.

Meanwhile, after developing her skills as an anthropologist, she wrote her second volume of folklore, *Tell My Horse,* published in 1938. It was largely ignored at the time because of taboos associated with the subject, but it is the most comprehensive look at voodoo in Jamaica and Haiti. During the 1940s and 1950s, Hurston suffered a quiet period because the naturalism of Richard Wright's novels and Ann Petry's feminist-naturalism supplanted her popular folk voice. Though even in this "quiet" period she published her autobiography, *Dust Tracks on a Road* (1942); another novel, *Seraph on the Suwanee* (1948); and several articles.

Modern audiences might have ignored Hurston's work, especially *Their Eyes Were Watching God,* had it not been for writer Alice Walker's revival of her material in the 1970s. Walker drew attention to Hurston's literary genius and feminism.

Much of the controversy over Hurston's fictional work centers on her rejection of the prevailing notion that Black culture is inferior and immoral. Additionally, Hurston rejected notions that women are subservient to men. These controversies caused her career to plummet, and she died poor and alone, in 1960.

Facing page: *Hurston's writing career began when her short story "Drenched in Light" was published in* Opportunity *magazine in December 1924.* Below: *Her hometown, Eatonville, Florida, was the setting for Hurston's most famous novel,* Their Eyes Were Watching God.

JESSE JACKSON

ONE OF THE NATION'S MOST IMPORTANT BLACK LEADERS, THE REV. JESSE JACKSON IS AN ELOQUENT, CHARISMATIC SPOKESMAN FOR ECONOMIC JUSTICE AND HUMAN RIGHTS IN AMERICA AND ABROAD. IN 1984 AND 1988, HE MADE SERIOUS BIDS TO BECOME PRESIDENT OF THE UNITED STATES, FINISHING SECOND IN 1988'S DEMOCRATIC PRIMARY. JACKSON CURRENTLY DIRECTS OPERATION PUSH AND THE NATIONAL RAINBOW COALITION.

Rev. Jesse Jackson has spent the last 35 years of public service in pursuit of economic justice and human rights for dispossessed Americans from all walks of life. He also has been instrumental in working for peace in various regions of the world. Jackson's activities have made him one of America's most important African-American leaders and an international statesman.

He is so firmly entrenched as a force for political and social change that in 1984 and again in 1988 he was able to make the most successful bid by a Black candidate in American history to become president of the United States. In 1984, Jackson captured over 3.5 million votes, 21 percent of the popular vote.

In 1988, Jackson, for a time, was the front-runner for the Democratic nomination after winning six southern states, the state of Michigan with 55 percent of the vote, and finishing second in Illinois. Though he eventually came in a strong second behind nominee Michael Dukakis, Jackson's bid attracted almost seven million voters—a

"rainbow coalition" from all across America. This allowed him to exert considerable power on the issues in the Democratic platform.

Being taken seriously as a presidential candidate was quite a rise from Jackson's humble origins. He was born October 8, 1941, in Greenville, South Carolina, to a 17-year-old unwed high school mother. They, along with his stepfather, lived in a three-room cottage with no indoor plumbing until he was in sixth grade. This environment may have produced in Jackson a strong need to prove himself and to succeed.

President of his high school class, Jackson won a college athletic scholarship to the University of Illinois, but racism there led him to return to North Carolina A&T College, where he became class president. He attended Chicago Theological Seminary and was ordained as a Baptist minister in 1968.

Jackson joined the Civil Rights Movement while at North Carolina A&T, and, in 1965, during demonstrations in Selma, Alabama, he became an aide to Dr. Martin Luther King, Jr. King appointed Jackson head of Operation

Breadbasket in Chicago in 1966. As the economic arm of King's Southern Christian Leadership Conference, Breadbasket used boycotts and selective buying strategies to induce White-owned businesses to carry Black-produced products and to hire Black workers.

In 1971, Jackson left the organization to found Operation PUSH (People United to Save Humanity), which expanded the economic mission of Breadbasket into the social and political arenas as well.

In 1984, Jackson also founded the National Rainbow Coalition to address the problems of the disenfranchised. In July 1990, he was elected "shadow senator" to try to attain statehood for the District of Columbia. He was sworn into office in January 1991.

As he continues these activities, Jackson also mentors his son Jesse Jackson, Jr., who in 1995 was elected Representative from Illinois's Second Congressional District.

Left: *Jackson has often traveled to crisis spots around the world and negotiated for the release of hostages.* Right: *Jackson speaks at a rally in the 1970s.*

JACK JOHNSON

In the early 20th century, when race relations were at one of the lowest points in history and lynchings and race riots occurred with regularity, John Arthur "Jack" Johnson became boxing's first Black heavyweight champion of the world.

In 1908, Johnson won the title with a vicious beating of Canadian Tommy Burns.

For 13 rounds, Johnson kept up a running conversation with Burns, even as he was dismantling him. Though bloodied, Burns would not quit. Finally, police entered the ring in the 14th round to stop the fight.

The new champion became an instant hero to most of Black America and a despised foe for much of White America, whose boasts of superiority over Blacks in all areas were shattered.

Fanning the flames of hatred for Johnson was the fact that he was an arrogant figure in the ring and out—he swaggered, wore flashy clothes and jewelry, had six cars and a large entourage, and displayed a penchant for openly romancing and often marrying White women.

As a result, the boxing community came up with a succession of "Great White Hopes" to try and dethrone this "uppity" Black fighter. Though controversial, Johnson was also one of the greatest boxers in history. He fought professionally from 1897 to 1928 and boxed in exhibitions as late as 1945. In those 48 years in the ring, he fought 114 bouts and was KOed only three times.

Born on March 31, 1878, in Galveston, Texas, Johnson quit school after fifth grade and worked a variety of odd jobs, including longshoring on the city's docks, which helped build his muscle strength. Despite his parents' objections, he began training as a boxer. After several amateur events, Johnson turned professional in 1897 at the age of 19, when he stood over six feet in height and weighed 180 pounds.

By 1901, Johnson was the best Black boxer in Texas and began successfully boxing across the country. After winning the "Negro" heavyweight championship in 1903, he demanded to fight Jim Jeffries, the reigning White champion. Jeffries decided to retire rather than demean himself by fighting a Black man, though he later did fight Johnson.

Tommy Burns won the vacated title, and financial considerations led him to fight Johnson. When Johnson humiliated Burns, Jeffries was lured out of retirement as the major White hope to defeat him. Johnson's 15th-round knockout of Jeffries in 1910 lead to several deadly race riots around the country.

Johnson was convicted in 1913 of violating the Mann Act for transporting his girlfriend, later his wife, across state lines for unlawful purposes. He was sentenced to a year in jail. He and his wife fled to Canada, then to France.

Johnson defended his title until 1915, when he lost it in a 26th-round knockout by Jess Willard in Cuba. Controversy still reigns about the outcome; there is speculation that Johnson "threw" the fight hoping the government would drop charges against him. He continued to fight exhibitions around the world and revel in his flamboyant lifestyle until June 10, 1946, when he died in a car crash.

Left: *In addition to boxing, this colorful figure also appeared in circuses, carnivals, and in special exhibitions demonstrating his strength.* Right: *Johnson enters the ring in 1931 at the age of 53, in the first of a series of boxing exhibitions he held throughout the country.*

JAMES WELDON JOHNSON

AN ACCOMPLISHED MAN OF LETTERS, JAMES WELDON JOHNSON HELPED ADVANCE THE CAUSE OF AFRICAN AMERICANS THROUGH HIS LITERARY AND MUSICAL CONTRIBUTIONS, AND WITH A 10-YEAR STINT AS HEAD OF THE NAACP. HE ALSO WROTE THE BLACK NATIONAL ANTHEM "LIFT EVERY VOICE AND SING."

James Weldon Johnson had a storied and varied life. He elevated the advancement of Blacks in America through his literary, musical, and educational contributions, his organizational accomplishments with the NAACP, and his service as a diplomat and U.S. counsel to foreign nations.

Johnson was a conservative man who believed in racial assimilation. Like his friend Booker T. Washington, he considered it the major responsibility of Blacks to lift themselves up by their own bootstraps. Johnson believed that to remove the label of "inferior," Blacks needed to prove their intellectual and physical equality.

Johnson was a true Renaissance man—historian, novelist, poet, educator. He excelled in all his endeavors. His accomplishments made him the most popular leader in the African-American community in his day behind Washington himself.

Johnson is best known for writing the lyrics to "Lift Every Voice and Sing," which is considered the Black National Anthem. Also, his 10-year stint as head of the NAACP was during a period when the organization experienced tremendous growth.

Johnson was born on June 17, 1871, in Jacksonville, Florida. His mother encouraged him and his brother, John, in music, art, and literature. But there was no high school for Blacks in Jacksonville, so James moved to Atlanta to complete his education through college.

After college, Johnson returned to Jacksonville and established courses that would lead to a high school degree for Blacks. He then became principal of that high school. He also studied law and became the first Black lawyer to pass the Florida bar in 1898.

The racial climate at the time led Johnson and his brother to move to New York in 1902. While there, they were successful in writing musical comedies and they penned a string of 200 songs for the Broadway stage.

While in New York, Johnson studied literature at Columbia University. He also began a growing interest in politics. In 1904, he became treasurer of New York City's Colored Republican Club and developed an association with Booker T. Washington.

At the urging of Booker T. Washington, President Teddy Roosevelt appointed Johnson U.S. counsel to Venezuela in 1906 and to Nicaragua in 1908. His consular positions gave Johnson enough free time to pursue writing. In 1912, he published *The Autobiography of an Ex-Colored Man,* one of the first accounts of a Black passing for White. He also became an editor and a popular columnist for the *New York Age* in 1914.

Johnson believed success in the literary and arts fields, as well as politics, by African Americans would help break down racial barriers. He became an advocate and literary critic of Black artistic works and compiled such pioneering anthologies as *The Book of American Negro Poetry* and *The Book of American Negro Spirituals*. In *Black Manhattan*, Johnson promoted Harlem as the center of Black culture during the famed Harlem Renaissance.

His works of poetry included two collections—*Fifty Years & Other Poems* and the book for which he is most remembered, *God's Trombones*. The last book is a group of sermons that are written in verse using Black vernacular.

In 1916, W.E.B. Du Bois urged Johnson to accept an offer to become a national organizer for the NAACP. Johnson was particularly successful in opening new branches in the South.

In 1920, he became executive secretary of the NAACP, the first African American to hold that post. For the next decade, Johnson was one of the most prominent Black leaders of his time .

In recognition of his large body of literary work, Johnson was appointed to the Adam K. Spence Chair of Creative Literature and Writing at Fisk University in October 1930. He resigned from the NAACP in December of that year. Working at the university allowed him to write, travel, lecture, and mentor other promising African Americans.

Johnson died an untimely death on June 26, 1938, when a train struck his car during a blinding rainstorm at an unguarded railroad crossing.

Historian, novelist, poet, educator, diplomat, lawyer, musician, lyricist, administrator, literary critic, editor, newspaper columnist, field organizer—Johnson's versatility and ability to excel at all of his endeavors made him one of the foremost leaders of his day.

JOHN H. JOHNSON

JOHN H. JOHNSON

HAS BEEN A PUBLISHING MAGNATE FOR MORE THAN 50 YEARS WITH HIS EBONY AND JET MAGAZINES, WHICH HAVE MADE HIM ONE OF THE RICHEST BLACK MEN IN AMERICA. ADMITTED TO NUMEROUS HALLS OF FAME, HE ALSO SITS ON THE BOARDS OF MAJOR AMERICAN CORPORATIONS AND INSTITUTIONS.

By sheer strength of will and determination, John H. Johnson rose from the poverty he experienced as a child in rural Arkansas to become one of the richest Black men in the nation. He founded and runs the Johnson Publishing Company empire, which for decades was by far the largest Black business in American history.

Since 1945, Johnson has published *Ebony* magazine, a lifestyle and general interest publication for Black America, which has a circulation of almost two million copies a month and is the crown jewel of his business. Johnson's second gold mine is *Jet*, a pocket-sized weekly magazine that has provided news to the Black community since 1951.

Other facets of his business conglomerate include *EM: Ebony Man* magazine, Fashion Fair Cosmetics, and the Ebony Fashion Fair. Johnson has also owned radio stations, an insurance company, extensive real estate, a mail-order firm, and a nationally syndicated TV show. He has also published several other magazines, which have had lives of varying lengths. His combined businesses have given Johnson a net worth of $150 million (as of 1989).

John Harold Johnson was born January 19, 1918, in Arkansas City, Arkansas, which had no public high school for Blacks. After taking eighth grade twice, his mother brought him to Chicago in 1933 to continue his education.

The ridicule he suffered at school because of his tattered clothes intensified Johnson's efforts to succeed. He pushed himself to become student council president and editor of the school newspaper. He was also a honor student.

In 1933, Harry Pace, president of Supreme Life Insurance Company, then the largest Black business in America, met young John at an Urban League dinner. He gave Johnson a job so that he could afford college. Johnson attended Northwestern and the University of Chicago, but dropped out to work full-time as Pace's personal assistant. (He eventually bought Pace's company.)

Part of his job was to give Pace a weekly briefing on news events of interest to Blacks, which gave Johnson the idea of developing a

magazine to deliver such news to the Black community at large.

When no one would back his idea, he borrowed $500, using his mother's furniture as collateral. With the money, he paid for a mailing to Supreme Insurance's client list seeking prepaid subscriptions to his newly proposed magazine.

The mailing produced enough subscriptions for Johnson to publish his first issue of *Negro Digest* in November 1942. By the end of 1943, the magazine had a circulation of 50,000; circulation had doubled after an October col-

umn written by First Lady Eleanor Roosevelt that same year. In November 1945, Johnson was able to launch *Ebony*, which provides positive role models and stories of Black success. The magazine immediately sold out its initial 25,000-copy press run.

Johnson still runs his empire as chairman of the board. Day-to-day operations are now handled by his daughter, Linda Johnson Rice, whom "The Publisher" (as he is called by his friends and associates) named president and chief operating officer of Johnson Publishing Company in 1989.

SCOTT JOPLIN

The raucous, intoxicating music form that was the worldwide rage from the turn of the century until about 1917 was largely the result of the work of Scott Joplin. Others may have called ragtime "jig piano," but Joplin preferred the term "syncopated piano music," thank you.

Joplin was born November 24, 1868, in Texarkana, Texas. His father was an ex-slave who played the fiddle and deserted the family early in Joplin's life. His mother was freeborn and she played the banjo. While growing up in a musical household, Joplin showed improvisational talent on the keyboard at an early age. Once his father left, Joplin's mother gave him the music lessons that he needed. She did this despite raising six children by herself. His mother took him along to houses where she did domestic work, so that Joplin could hone his skills practicing on pianos in those family parlors.

Joplin's talent, especially in improvisation, soon led him to become the talk of the area among Blacks and even several Whites. Capable volunteers instructed him in formal piano and harmony. They also instilled in the young man a lifelong interest in music education.

In the mid-1880s, in part to ease the burden on his mother, Joplin left Texarkana. He wandered as an itinerant piano player, becoming a "professa" (a pianist who plays by memory) in the world of honky-tonks and bordellos. It was here that he learned to rag. But he also played in churches, at respected "socials," and in vaudeville with a group called the Texas Medley Quartette (which originally had five members and then reorganized with eight members).

In 1894, Joplin settled in Sedalia, Missouri, attending the George R. Smith College for Negroes. Here he took courses in music composition and harmony. He also resumed his professa-ship at Sedalia's Maple Leaf Club.

Once his major compositions began to be published, in 1899, the richness, originality, and painstaking craftsmanship that marked Joplin's music garnered great appreciation. It also established him as more than a ragtime hack.

His "Maple Leaf Rag" sold more than a million copies of sheet music at the time of publication and fueled the ragtime explosion in popular music. The song earned Joplin the title King of Ragtime and brought him the financial security to break away from the honky-tonk circuit.

He continued to produce great rag piano works, such as "The Entertainer," which was immortalized in the popular 1973 film *The Sting.* Joplin began turning to different forms of music composition that brought him less success and more depression.

He produced a folk ballet called *The Ragtime Dance* in 1899 and then a ragtime opera in 1903 called *A Guest of Honor,* which received lukewarm public reaction at best. In fact, he went broke trying to stage *A Guest of Honor* on an unsuccessful tour. This forced Joplin to return to creating rags, which were always a source of commercial and financial success for him.

He tried another attempt at serious music with the opera *Treemonisha,* an ode to his mother, which he published in 1911. Repeated unsuccessful attempts to mount a full-scale production of the opera caused Joplin increasingly severe bouts of depression. Over the next five years, his mental deterioration progressed rapidly until the autumn of 1916, when he was committed to the Manhattan State Hospital. He died there on April 1, 1917.

Ironically, because of the interest in Joplin and ragtime in the 1970s, he has received the status of a serious classical composer. In 1970, a classical label released a collection of his rags performed by classical musician Joshua Rifkin. After the New York City Library published a two-volume set in 1971 called *The Collected Works of Scott Joplin,* classical artists began regularly including his compositions in their concert performances. The movie *The Sting* also popularized several of his rags.

Even his beloved *Treemonisha* was revived, first in concert form by the Atlanta Symphony and then in a full-blown production by the Houston Grand Opera in 1975. Finally, Joplin was issued a special Pulitzer Prize in 1976 and his likeness was put on a commemorative U.S. postage stamp in 1983.

Joplin's legacy includes 32 ragtime piano solos, 7 rags in collaboration with others, 9 songs, 2 syncopated waltzes, 2 operas, 1 instruction book, 2 arrangements, and 11 miscellaneous works. There are also 11 surviving unpublished manuscripts. Several more of his works are probably lost. Some people believe Joplin destroyed them himself because they didn't meet his rigorous standards.

MICHAEL JORDAN

No one ever played the game of basketball as fluently as Michael Jordan, nicknamed "Air" because of his extraordinary ability to float off the ground longer than seemingly possible in order to perform his scoring magic. The Chicago Bulls's acrobatic shooting guard led the team to four National Basketball Association (NBA) championships from 1991 to 1993, and 1996.

The strength of his game is his completeness as a player. With no weakness, Jordan is equally adept at scoring, defending, passing, and rebounding. Coupled with his limitless physical talents are an intense focus, fierce determination, inspired leadership, and biting sense of competition.

The records, awards, and achievements collected by "His Airness" are a testament to his greatness: Most Valuable Player for four seasons (1988, 1991, 1992, 1996), in four NBA Finals (1991 to 1993, 1996), and two All-Star Games (1988, 1996); Defensive Player of the Year in 1988; and Rookie of the Year in 1985. He also helped the United States win two Olympic gold medals (1984, 1992).

Attesting to his all-around game, Jordan was named to the All-NBA first team for seven straight years (1987 to 1993) and the All-Defensive first team six straight years (1988 to 1993). He was the second player in league history (along with Wilt Chamberlain) to win seven straight scoring titles (1987 to 1993). He also won that title in 1996, making him the record holder for the title.

Jordan's a virtual scoring machine. He is the Bulls's all-time leader, with more than 24,000 points so far. Jordan's personal highs include 69 points against Cleveland in 1990 and a playoff-record 63 points against Boston in 1986. He's scored 50 or more points 35 times and set an NBA record for consecutive points with 23 scored against Atlanta in 1987.

Jordan holds the career record for scoring in All-Star Games at 21.9 points (he's played in nine of them) and the career scoring average in the playoffs at 34.4 points.

In the 1993 NBA Finals against Phoenix, Jordan set records for highest scoring average at 41 points, most total points at 246, and most baskets made at 101. In the 1992 Finals

against Portland, Jordan scored 35 points in the first half of Game 1, setting a finals record; his six three-point baskets in that half tied another record.

Born February 17, 1963, in Brooklyn, New York, Jordan grew up in Wilmington, North Carolina. In 1993, after the Bulls' third championship and the murder of his father, James Jordan, Michael retired from the sport for a year and a half to rest and play professional baseball.

But after batting only .202 as a minor leaguer, Jordan returned to basketball late in the 1994–95 season. In 1996, he led the Bulls to an NBA-record 72-game winning season.

Jordan's efforts are not all on the basketball court, though. In an era where sports stars are no longer heroes, he has remained an example to children. Through a self-named foundation run by his mother, he has worked to help underprivileged kids. Though he is disbanding the foundation, he plans to continue his work with inner-city children and donating to other charities.

Left: *Jordan received his fourth MVP trophy for his unbelievable, record-setting 1996 season.* Right: *Jordan demonstrates his amazing ability to soar through the air.*

MAULANA KARENGA

"MAULANA" RON KARENGA CREATED THE KWANZAA CULTURAL HOLIDAY FOR PEOPLE OF AFRICAN DESCENT IN 1966. THE SEVEN PRINCIPLES CELEBRATED DURING THE FESTIVAL ARE UNITY, SELF-DETERMINATION, COLLECTIVE WORK AND RESPONSIBILITY, COOPERATIVE ECONOMICS, PURPOSE, CREATIVITY, AND FAITH. KARENGA IS CHAIRMAN OF THE BLACK STUDIES DEPARTMENT AT CALIFORNIA STATE UNIVERSITY AT LONG BEACH.

For the past 30 years, in the last week of December, African Americans have celebrated the increasingly popular cultural holiday known as Kwanzaa. The ritual, a combination of ancient African traditions fused with the newer traditions of Black Americans, was created in 1966 by Dr. Ron Karenga, chairman of the Black Studies Department at California State University at Long Beach. Karenga is known by the title of "Maulana," a Swahili word meaning master-teacher.

Kwanzaa celebrates seven principles—one each day of the holiday—that are rooted in African history and which were selected by Karenga as keys to building the Black family, community, and culture.

The principles, called *Nguzo Saba,* include *umoja* (unity), *kujichagulia* (self-determination), *ujima* (collective work and responsibility), *ujamaa* (cooperative economics), *nia* (purpose), *kuumba* (creativity), and *imani* (faith). The holiday begins on December 26 and concludes on January 1, as *kwanzaa* itself means first—Africans have historically held celebrations at

the occasion of the first harvests of the year. In the spirit of *umoja* (unity), Karenga deliberately selected the terms from the common Swahili language, which represents all of Africa instead of any particular group or tribe. He wanted the Kwanzaa festival to be celebrated by all people of African descent in America and throughout the world, regardless of their individual religious and political beliefs and practices.

Karenga also created the popular red, black, and green flag as a symbol of the Kwanzaa celebration: red for the struggle, black for the people, green for their hope. The idea of the holiday caught on during the Black Power days of the Civil Rights Movement, as African Americans gained a heightened awareness of their heritage and their culture. Kwanzaa has become ingrained in American culture ever since.

Born in Maryland in 1941, Karenga holds two Ph.D.s from the University of California at Los Angeles, one in social ethics, the other in political science. As a doctoral candidate in 1965, Karenga founded the United Slaves (US)

Facing page: *Karenga is a regular on the national lecture and Black Studies conferences circuits, speaking on the lasting effects of slavery on African Americans.* Left: *A Black nationalist, Karenga's writings have covered subjects ranging from feminism to Pan-Africanism, to Black art and culture.*

Cultural Organization following the riots in Watts in Los Angeles.

Karenga believed that the key to helping Black Americans was rescuing and reconstructing their original African culture and using it as a foundation to learn about and help understand who they are. While he was with US, Karenga created Kwanzaa, after researching African cultures throughout history.

US disbanded in 1974, while Karenga was serving a four-year sentence on a controversial charge of assaulting one of the group's members. He used the time to begin a writing career. Since his parole in 1975, Karenga has written eight books, including *Introduction to Black Studies*, which is a staple of African-American studies programs in colleges and universities.

MARTIN LUTHER KING, JR.

DR. MARTIN LUTHER KING,
*JR., WAS A PROMINENT CIVIL
RIGHTS LEADER WHO REMAINS
THE MOST OUTSTANDING SYMBOL
OF THAT MOVEMENT, WHICH LED
TO VOTING RIGHTS FOR AFRICAN
AMERICANS, AND AN END TO LEGAL
EMPLOYMENT DISCRIMINATION
AND SEGREGATION OF PUBLIC
FACILITIES. KING WON THE
NOBEL PEACE PRIZE IN
1964 AND HIS BIRTHDAY IS NOW
A NATIONAL HOLIDAY.*

The Reverend Dr. Martin Luther King, Jr., was the leading organizer of the Civil Rights Movement of the 1950s and 1960s, which led to the abolition of legal discrimination against African Americans in employment, desegregation of public places, and voting rights for Blacks.

King's success came from elevating the issue of equality into a moral crusade. He appealed to the conscience of the nation and brought pressure on the federal government to pass legislation that remedied many of society's inequities.

The strategy employed by the self-described "drum major" for peace and justice was nonviolent direct action protests—including demonstrations, sit-ins, pray-ins, marches, and boycotts. These drew attention to discrimination.

This eloquent, stirring orator was able to convince people of goodwill that justice is inherent in the civil rights cause. He galvanized Blacks into actions that were fraught with danger; indeed, actions that cost King his own life when he was assassinated in 1968 at the age of 39.

But his courageous vision and dedication earned him the nation's highest accolades, including the NAACP's Spingarn Medal in 1957; the Nobel Peace Prize in 1964—he was the youngest recipient and only the second Black so honored; and the Presidential Medal of Freedom in 1977. King became the first Black American to be named *Time* magazine's "Man of the Year" in 1964, and, in 1986, Congress designated his birthday a national holiday.

King was born on January 15, 1929, in Atlanta, Georgia, into a family of Black ministers. At age 15, he was accepted into Morehouse College under a program for gifted students and he received his bachelor's degree in sociology at age 19.

Admitted into Crozer Theological Seminary in Chester, Pennsylvania, King graduated first in his class and was the first Black student body president. On a fellowship to Boston University, he received his Ph.D. in systematic theology in 1955. While there, he met and married Coretta Scott.

After college, King accepted the pastorship at Dexter Avenue Baptist Church in Montgomery, Alabama. In December 1955, a Black

seamstress named Rosa Parks was arrested for refusing to give her seat to a White man on a Montgomery bus.

Black citizens of the town decided to challenge the city's law requiring segregated bus seating: They formed the Montgomery Improvement Association, with King as head, to take action.

Lawsuits were filed and for more than a year Blacks refused to ride the buses. They walked, carpooled, took taxis, and found other transportation. Though King's home was bombed, the boycott forced the bus company to desegregate and in late 1956, the Supreme Court declared the bus segregation law unconstitutional.

Afterward, King traveled extensively and lectured about civil rights for Blacks. In India in 1959, he studied Mahatma Ghandi's ideas of nonviolent resistance. He used those ideas when he assumed the presidency of the Southern Christ-

Facing page: *King is generally acknowledged to be one of the great social leaders in world history. His work and his legacy live on through the Center For Nonviolent Social Change in Atlanta, which was established by Coretta King, following King's death.* Left: *King's writings help explain the philosophies by which he directed the Civil Rights Movement. Those works include the books* Stride Toward Freedom: The Montgomery Story *(1958),* Why We Can't Wait *(1964), and* Where Do We Go from Here: Chaos or Community *(1967). He also wrote one of America's greatest essays, "Letter from a Birmingham Jail," in 1963.*

Above: *King greets well-wishers on August 28, 1963, after delivering his famous "I Have a Dream" speech at the foot of the Lincoln Memorial during the March on Washington, D.C. King began the speech by emphasizing the lack of progress made by African Americans in securing the rights that had been promised in Lincoln's Emancipation Proclamation.* Facing page: *In June 1967, King gives a press conference with his aides (from right) Bernard Lee, Al Raby, and Mike Lawson in attendance. King was expanding the scope of his efforts to cover human rights, as well as civil rights.*

ian Leadership Conference in 1960. For the next five years, King's use of nonviolent direct action campaigns throughout the South captured the country's sympathy because of the brutality directed at protesters.

In the spring of 1963, as demonstrators sought to end segregation in downtown Birmingham stores, city officials used attack dogs and fire hoses against unarmed men, women, and children. Hundreds of marchers were jailed, including King, who was placed in solitary confinement. While there, he wrote his famous "Letter from a Birmingham Jail," which explained why he believed in nonviolent direct action. The letter is considered one of

the greatest essays in American history. TV coverage of the Birmingham atrocity stunned the nation. The resulting negative reaction forced White business owners to agree to Movement demands.

In August 1963, King and other Movement leaders staged the March on Washington, D.C., where more than 200,000 people gathered to support passage of civil rights legislation. King gave his "I Have a Dream" speech and met with President Kennedy. The Civil Rights Act was passed the next year.

Another bloody confrontation occurred in Selma, Alabama, in 1965, on a march to Montgomery in support of Black voting rights. When protesters were turned back by law enforcement using tear gas and nightsticks, national outrage caused religious leaders of all denominations to join a second attempted march. Afterward, President Lyndon Johnson maneuvered the Voting Rights Act of 1965 through Congress.

After these successes, King's efforts turned toward organizing a multiracial Poor People's Campaign to march on Washington, D.C., to secure basic economic rights. The demonstration was planned for the spring of 1968, but in April, while in Memphis, King was killed by sniper James Earl Ray.

In 1986, Spike Lee enjoyed huge commercial success with his first major film, *She's Gotta Have It.* Lee proved that well-told stories from the Black experience could be profitable and attract diverse audiences.

Born Shelton Jackson Lee on March 20, 1957, in Atlanta, and nicknamed "Spike" by his mother, Lee grew up in the Brooklyn section of New York City with an early interest in the arts. His father is noted jazz musician Bill Lee; his late mother, Jacquelyn, took the youngster to plays, museums, and galleries.

As a student at Morehouse College, Lee took an interest in filmmaking, which led to a summer internship at Columbia Pictures in 1979 following his graduation. He entered New York University's film school and for his master's thesis, made the hour-long comedy, *Joe's Bed-Stuy Barbershop: We Cut Heads,* about a Brooklyn barbershop fronting for the local numbers racket.

The film won a student Academy Award from the Academy of Motion Picture Arts and Sciences in 1982 and was received with critical acclaim at film festivals from San Francisco to Switzerland. However, with no offers from the Hollywood film industry to continue his budding career, Lee decided to produce his movies independently.

Four years later, in 1986, he was able to complete *She's Gotta Have It,* which was shot in 12 days in a small Brooklyn apartment and nearby park. Financing was a major problem. Lee started with only $18,000 and throughout production kept asking everyone he could for any money they could spare.

The film, about the hectic love life of an independent young African-American woman, was completed for a relatively paltry $175,000, but went on to gross over $7 million. For his efforts, Lee won the prize for the best new film at the Cannes International Film Festival and received the Los Angeles

SPIKE LEE'S SUCCESS AS A FILMMAKER HAS OPENED THE DOORS OF THE MOVIE INDUSTRY FOR A NEW GROUP OF YOUNG AFRICAN-AMERICAN DIRECTORS. LEE'S MOVIES ATTEMPT TO PORTRAY THE RICHNESS OF BLACK LIFE AND CULTURE ACCURATELY AND WITHOUT STEREOTYPES. HE IS BEST KNOWN FOR DO THE RIGHT THING, JUNGLE FEVER, AND MALCOLM X.

Film Critics Award for best new director in 1986. The film was also named to many critics top ten lists for 1986.

Columbia Pictures picked up Lee's second major film release, *School Daze,* a musical about life at a Black college, for $6 million. The movie made *Variety*'s weekly list of the top ten moneymaking films in March 1988. His third release, *Do the Right Thing,* about racial tensions between Italian Americans and African Americans one hot summer day, became a mainstream hit and cemented Lee's reputation as a bona fide major American filmmaker. Lee was nominated for an Academy award for his original screenplay.

Lee's movies, though controversial, continue to be box office magic. He has gone on to make *Mo' Better Blues, Jungle Fever, Malcolm X, Crooklyn, Clockers, Girl 6,* and is currently at work on *Get on the Bus!* (working title), the story of a group of men going to 1995's Million Man March on Washington, D.C.

Left: *One of Lee's pet projects in the works is his second biography of a famous African American, baseball's Jackie Robinson.* Right: *Lee is as recognized for his acting roles and TV commercials as he is for being a filmmaker. He is pictured on the set of* Crooklyn.

ALAIN LOCKE

DR. ALAIN LOCKE

CAME FROM A FAMILY WHERE EDUCATION WAS A TRADITION. HE BECAME THE FIRST AFRICAN-AMERICAN RHODES SCHOLAR AND THE ONLY BLACK RECIPIENT OF THE SCHOLARSHIP FOR THE DURATION OF HIS LIFETIME. HEAD OF HOWARD UNIVERSITY'S PHILOSOPHY DEPARTMENT, LOCKE WAS ALSO THE LEADING INTELLECTUAL SPOKESMAN FOR THE HARLEM RENAISSANCE.

In 1907, Dr. Alain Locke had the distinction of becoming the first African-American Rhodes Scholar, earning the academic world's highest honor. He remained the only Black recipient of the scholarship during his lifetime.

It's not difficult to imagine Locke's achievement, considering the intellectual genes coursing through his veins, in addition to his environmental conditioning. With teachers throughout his family tree, it is not surprising that he became a widely respected educator and intellectual.

Born September 13, 1885, in Philadelphia, Locke contracted rheumatic fever as a child, which left him with permanent heart damage. He adjusted to the limitations by burying himself in books and the arts.

Locke graduated second in his high school class, then studied at the Philadelphia School of Pedagogy. He finished first in his class there. After entering Harvard University, he completed the four-year program in only three years. He graduated Phi Beta Kappa and magna cum laude in 1907.

As a Rhodes Scholar, Locke spent three years studying philosophy at Oxford, where he founded the African Union Society. After attending the University of Berlin from 1910 to 1911, he returned to the States and received his Ph.D. in philosophy from Harvard in 1918.

Locke began teaching at Howard University in 1912, and he taught for almost 40 years until his retirement in 1953 as head of Howard's philosophy department. During his tenure, he reformed Howard's liberal arts program, and Locke's stature as an education reformer was respected nationwide. He also advocated the creation of an African Studies Program, but that was not implemented until 1954.

In 1925, Locke edited an anthology called *The New Negro.* It contained social essays, fic-

JOE LOUIS, A HEAVYWEIGHT BOXING CHAMPION DURING THE DEPRESSION AND WORLD WAR II, EMERGED WHEN ALL AMERICANS NEEDED A HERO. THE FACT HE WAS BLACK MADE HIM THAT MUCH MORE LOVABLE TO MANY. THE FACT HE OPENED UP PROFESSIONAL SPORTS TO OTHER AFRICAN AMERICANS MAKES HIM IMMORTAL.

Joe Louis Barrow, the son of Alabama sharecroppers, was born in 1914 at the beginning of World War I. By World War II, he would become known as the Brown Bomber and remembered as perhaps the greatest prizefighter this country has ever known.

After moving from the Deep South to Detroit at age 12, Louis's mother had visions of him becoming a great violinist. But after only a few lessons, he left music. Then, a friend who was a 1932 Golden Gloves champion invited him to the gym to work out as his sparring partner. Louis accepted and landed a right punch that almost knocked his friend out of the ring. From then on, as his friend stated, Louis's violin days were gone.

In 1935, after a sensational string of early victories, Louis finally faced a major opponent—former world heavyweight champion Primo Carnera, an Italian. To many, Carnera represented the Fascist ambitions of Italian dictator Benito Mussolini, who was on the verge of invading Ethiopia. Louis was an African American who symbolized the free world and also the pride of the African people, since Ethiopia was the world's oldest Black independent nation. Holding a record crowd the night of the fight, Yankee Stadium was filled with mostly Blacks and Italians. By the sixth round, the gigantic Italian stallion was soundly defeated.

In June 1936, Louis faced another opponent who was seen as a symbol of Aryan supremacy—Max Schmeling, the German former heavyweight champion. It was a great fight. In the 12th round, Schmeling knocked out the Brown Bomber.

Louis came back in 1937 to recapture the title from James J. Braddock with an eighth-round knockout. In 1938, he faced Schmeling for a rematch that would take on international

tion, poetry, and dramatic and music criticism of the day. This period became known as the Harlem Renaissance, which was characterized by pride in Black culture.

His reputation brought him to the attention of White cultural institutions and patrons and through them, Locke was able to boost the careers of such literary luminaries as Langston Hughes and Zora Neale Hurston.

Between 1936 and 1942, Locke edited the "Bronze Booklets" series, which detailed cultural and scholarly achievements and progressive views of Black life. For two decades, he reviewed and wrote about Black literature and art. His numerous essays on Black culture and its dramatic upsurge during the Harlem Renaissance led to Locke's recognition as the foremost authority in the field. Among his many other accomplishments, Locke was also a respected collector of African art.

Locke died on June 9, 1954, in New York, from his recurring heart problems.

Left: *When Locke became a Rhodes Scholar, it dramatically dampened the arguments of many White American academians who believed that Blacks were intellectually inferior.* Right: *Because of his academic success, Locke became a symbol of intellectual achievement among African Americans.*

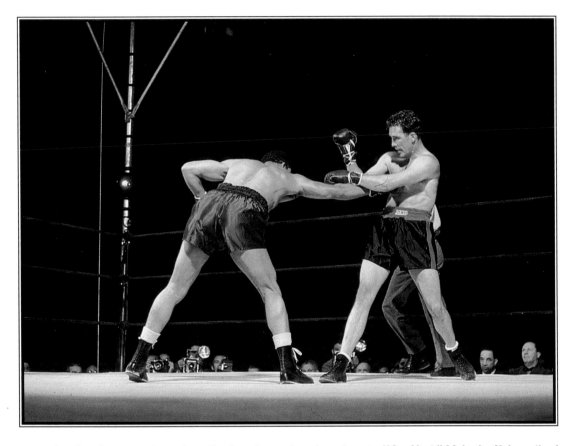

Facing page: *After being told that an upcoming opponent was "quick," the legendary Brown Bomber coined the phrase, "He can run, but he can't hide."* Left: *Louis meets Billy Conn in a rematch in 1946. Neither fighter had boxed, except in exhibitions, in over four years. Though both boxers appeared lethargic, Louis KOed Conn in round eight to retain his title.*

attention. In what some have described as the most anticipated fight of this century, Louis avenged himself and his race with a stunning first-round knockout in two minutes and four seconds. It delighted millions of Black radio listeners and raised the morale of other Americans who needed a lift during the bleakest of the Depression years. In Harlem alone, tens of thousands had a riotous celebration in the streets, chanting, "Joe Louis is the first American to KO a Nazi." Malcolm X described Louis's prominence this way: "Every Negro boy old enough to walk wanted to be the next Brown Bomber."

Louis went on to defend his title a record 25 times. By doing so, he became America's first African-American hero, destroying the myth of racial inferiority as soundly as he defeated his opponents in the ring. He died April 12, 1981, in Las Vegas.

THURGOOD MARSHALL

The man who would ultimately grow up to become America's first African-American Supreme Court justice was born in Baltimore in 1908. His father was a country club steward and Pullman car porter and his mother was a teacher. The judge's name was Thurgood Marshall.

For 25 years prior to joining the high court, Marshall was "the most important advocate for America," said his colleague Justice William J. Brennan, referring to Marshall's 29 winning arguments before the Supreme Court—a record that remains unmatched by any lawyer, Black or White.

Marshall's mother, who had considerable influence over him, traced her African roots to a 17th-century Congolese slave who caused so much trouble that his slave master finally set him free. Freedom would eventually become Thurgood Marshall's driving force, too.

Marshall's paternal grandfather was a freeman who enlisted in the Union Army during the Civil War. He took the first name "Thoroughgood" in order to satisfy Army regulations that every soldier must have a first and a last name.

During the Depression, Marshall attended Lincoln University in Pennsylvania and Howard University Law School, two of the best historically Black universities. He was a protégé of legal scholar Charles Houston, an NAACP attorney. Eventually, the NAACP would bring ten education cases before the Supreme Court and would be successful at ending segregation in all public schools.

In 1938, after Houston resigned from the NAACP as special counsel, Marshall succeeded him in the legal fight against Jim Crow segregation. Marshall argued the subtleties of the Fourteenth Amendment, winning a number of cases after he was appointed as special counsel to the NAACP's Legal Defense and Education Fund. Marshall's success rate would also win him the coveted NAACP Spingarn Medal in December 1946, for his distinguished service as a lawyer before the Supreme Court.

For the decade or so after Marshall took the helm, case after case dealing with segregation moved him closer to his goal of having the U.S. Supreme Court overturn a previous ruling, *Plessy* v. *Ferguson*, that declared that separate but equal was constitutional.

Finally, on May 17, 1954, after Marshall presented his side, the Supreme Court handed down its epic decision in *Brown* v. *Board of Education*. The ruling said that segregation in public schools was unconstitutional, and that separate but equal has no place in American society. Jim Crow segregation was dead.

But Marshall didn't just work for justice in the United States. During 1960, Marshall worked three months to draft the constitution for the soon-to-be independent republic of Kenya.

In September 1961, President Kennedy named Thurgood Marshall to the U.S. Second Circuit Court of Appeals. Kennedy did this despite his brother Robert's opposition, who feared that the appointment would upset southern politicos. At that time there was no other Black person working in the courthouse, not even as a clerk or a janitor.

Six years later, President Johnson selected Marshall to sit on the Supreme Court, making him the first African American to hold a high court seat. During his tenure on the bench, Marshall wrote the majority opin-

ion on many cases upholding civil rights and constitutional democracy.

Marshall served with great distinction until his retirement June 27, 1991. He was replaced on the bench by neo-conservative African-American judge Clarence Thomas. This choice did not sit well with Marshall. Shortly before he died, in 1993, he warned against "picking the wrong Negro," adding "there's no difference between a white snake and a black snake. They'll both bite...."

Facing page: *Marshall learned to perfect his arguments before the Supreme Court by assisting Charles Houston, his former Howard University law instructor and the NAACP's legal architect. Marshall successfully argued cases that would eventually lead to the end of public segregation in America.* Below: *Marshall speaks in a Black church in 1959, five years after his success in the* Brown v. Board of Education *case.*

OSCAR MICHEAUX

Oscar Micheaux may not have been the most gifted filmmaker in history, but he was as good a huckster as any Hollywood producer. Micheaux, one of the first and certainly most determined of African-American filmmakers, independently wrote, produced, directed, and distributed some 48 silent and sound feature films in the 30-year period between 1918 and 1948.

The films were mostly melodramas, Westerns, and crime films, but these all-Black productions were far more advanced than Hollywood movies in portraying African Americans as anything other than subservient and in demeaning roles.

Despite his affinity for genre movies, Micheaux attempted to address serious issues in a few of his films. *Within Our Gates* contains a sequence in which a character is lynched. *God's Stepchildren* concerns a light-skinned Black who tries to pass for White. Whenever he attempted this type of controversial material, he experienced problems with local censors.

Whether following the conventions of familiar genres or dealing with serious issues, Micheaux's movies did what movies are supposed to do—entertain. Millions of Blacks patronized his films in the segregated movie theaters of the day. White audiences even saw his movies at midnight showings.

Micheaux was born January 2, 1884, in rural Cairo, Illinois, one of 13 children of former slave parents. He left home at 17 to become a Pullman porter and, after working the Chicago to Portland route, became enchanted with life out West. In 1904, Micheaux purchased a homestead in South Dakota and by all accounts became a successful farmer.

To spread the word to city-dwelling Blacks back East about the opportunities waiting in the West, Micheaux began writing novels based on his own experiences. To sell his books, he took to barnstorming through Black communities in the South and West on promotional tours. He held meetings in churches, schools, and homes and sold directly to that clientele.

In 1918, a Black independent film company sought to buy the film rights to his novel *The Homesteader,* but Micheaux insisted that he be allowed to direct. When they refused, he refused. He raised funds from the same people he sold his books to in order to make the film himself. A moviemaking career was born.

Micheaux's filmmaking style was resourceful, to say the least. Always operating on a shoestring budget, he shot scenes only once, leaving in whatever miscues happened to be caught on camera, using mirrors to enhance whatever natural lighting happened to be available, and using existing buildings instead of constructing sets. These quickie features were generally finished in six weeks. Then Micheaux, a hefty six-footer, would storm from town to town, stirring demand to see his current movie and raising funds to make the next.

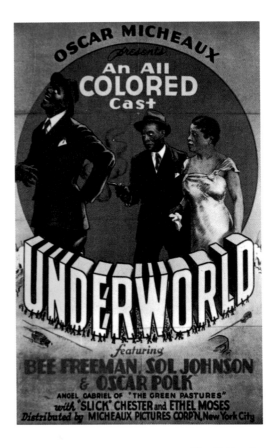

In 1931, Micheaux released *The Exile,* the first all-sound film produced by a Black company, and in 1948, his movie *The Betrayal* became the first African-American-made film to premiere on Broadway. *Body and Soul* (1925) is considered by some critics to be his best picture, and it offered Paul Robeson his movie debut.

Micheaux died April 1, 1951, while, appropriately enough, on a promotional tour.

Facing page: *Micheaux was admitted into the Screen Directors' Guild posthumously. His 1918 movie,* Birthright, *is generally considered to be the first full-length film made by an African American.* Left: *A promotional poster for Micheaux's movie* Underworld, *a crime drama. In addition to crime dramas, Micheaux's repertory included melodramas and Westerns.*

TONI MORRISON

In 1989, writer Toni Morrison, who won a Pulitzer Prize for her 1987 novel, Beloved, joined Princeton University as the Robert F. Goheen Professor in the Council of the Humanities. This made her the first Black woman writer in American history to hold a named chair at an Ivy League University. In 1993, she became the first African American to win the Nobel Prize in Literature.

Toni Morrison is one of the most important Black female writers in the nation's history and certainly one of the most significant novelists living today. Her primary focus has been on conveying the realities of life for Black women and the physical and economic violence that affects them, along with the culture of the larger Black community. Morrison's works have won the Pulitzer Prize and National Book Critics Circle Award, and she won the Nobel Prize in Literature in 1993.

Morrison has had a three-pronged career as writer, editor, and educator. Born Chloe Anthony Wofford on February 18, 1931, in Lorain, Ohio, she was an extremely intelligent child. Morrison was the only Black student in her first-grade class, and she learned to read before her classmates.

After graduating from high school with honors, she attended Howard University as an English major and began using the first name "Toni." Following her graduation in 1953, Morrison earned a master's degree in English from Cornell University in 1955 and began teaching in 1957 at Howard, where she had a short-lived marriage to architect Harold Morrison. Her students at Howard included activist Stokely Carmichael and Claude Brown, author of *Manchild in the Promised Land*.

In the mid-1960s, Morrison left Howard to work as an editor with Random House Books, and a few years later, was promoted to senior editor to work on Black fiction. She helped develop the writing careers of luminaries such as Angela Davis, Toni Cade Bambara, and Gayl Jones.

Morrison began writing more herself. In 1970, she turned an old short story into her first novel, *The Bluest Eye*, about a little Black girl who wants blue eyes. *Sula*, her second novel, is about an intensely individualistic Black woman and her relationships; it came out in 1973.

Morrison's third novel, *Song of Solomon*, about a middle-class Black man searching through slavery for his ancestral roots, won her the National Book Critics Circle Award when it debuted in 1977. A fourth novel, *Tar Baby*, stayed on best-seller lists for over three months and caused Morrison to be the first Black American woman to be featured on the cover of *Newsweek* magazine.

The author left Random House in the mid-1980s, after 20 years, to become the Albert Schweitzer Professor of Humanities at the State University of New York at Albany. While there, she wrote her finest work, *Beloved,* in 1987, which won the Pulitzer Prize for fiction.

Beloved is a monument to the millions of Black Americans who endured slavery. Morrison was inspired to create the work after reading the true story of Margaret Garner, who escaped to freedom in Ohio from slavery in Kentucky, along with her four children. Facing recapture, Garner killed one child and unsuccessfully attempted the same with two others rather than have them returned to lives as slaves.

Morrison recently published her sixth novel, *Jazz,* about a Harlem couple in the 1920s. She also released a scholarly volume of literary criticism titled *Playing in the Dark.* She continues to teach and write.

Left: *Morrison's third novel,* Song of Solomon, *won the National Book Critics Circle Award in 1977 and became the first novel by an African American to become a Book-of-the-Month Club selection since Richard Wright's* Native Son *in 1940. Right: Her fifth novel,* Beloved, *won the Pulitzer Prize for fiction in 1988.*

DURING ROBERT MOSES'S

BRIEF CIVIL RIGHTS CAREER, HE

SPENT FOUR DANGEROUS YEARS AS

FIELD SECRETARY FOR THE

MISSISSIPPI STUDENT

NONVIOLENT COORDINATING

COMMITTEE, FIGHTING TO

REGISTER BLACKS TO VOTE. HE

OPENED "FREEDOM SCHOOLS" TO

TEACH VOTER REGISTRATION AND

COMMUNITY ACTION STRATEGIES,

HELD MOCK ELECTIONS, AND

CHALLENGED THE STATE'S

SEGREGATED SLATE OF

DEMOCRATIC CONVENTION

DELEGATES.

Robert Moses played a brief but crucial role in the Civil Rights Movement. His efforts at voter registration for Blacks in Mississippi as a representative of the Student Nonviolent Coordinating Committee (SNCC) helped lead to the Voting Rights Act of 1965.

Born January 23, 1935, in Harlem, Moses earned his master's degree in philosophy from Harvard University and taught math in an elite private New York high school.

Stirred by the student sit-in movement of 1960, Moses went to Atlanta and joined SNCC, which was spearheading the protests. He became the first full-time SNCC worker in the Deep South, assigned to register Black voters

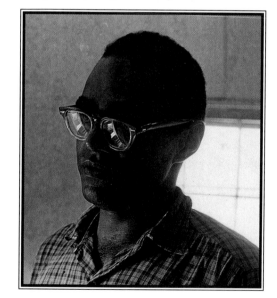

in Mississippi. His job was extremely dangerous and Moses was harassed, beaten, jailed, and almost killed.

In August 1961, he opened voter registration schools in two counties in southwest Mississippi. These schools taught Blacks how to register, the power of community action to combat injustices, and current events. In October, Moses was jailed for leading a protest march. When he was released in December, nearly all the Blacks he worked with had been intimidated into backing out of his registration efforts.

In the spring of 1962, SNCC joined with other Mississippi groups to create the Council of Federated Organizations (COFO), with Moses as head, to unify registration efforts in the state. In 1963, COFO staged the Freedom Election, a mock election open to all Black adults, to show the country how strongly the right to vote was desired by Blacks in Mississippi. More than 80,000 Blacks cast votes on the Freedom Ballot.

The success of that effort led Moses to create the 1964 Freedom Summer Project, in which 1,000 volunteers entered the state to set up "freedom" schools and centers to work on voter registration. The summer was violent—there were a reported 35 shootings,

Facing page: *Moses was a quiet, courageous organizer who shunned the leadership limelight that he was pulled into. He left the Civil Rights Movement after a few years, but made a significant impact in securing voting rights for African Americans.* Left: *Moses (left) with fellow organizers in Cleveland, Mississippi, in 1962, about the time the Council of Federated Organizations was established to unify voter registration efforts in the state.*

80 beatings, 60 bombings, and well over 1,000 arrests. Under such conditions, very few Blacks were registered, but the project gained national attention.

During the same summer, Moses helped create the Mississippi Freedom Democratic Party (MFDP) to challenge the segregated Mississippi Democratic Party for seats at the 1964 Democratic National Convention. More than 60,000 people registered as members.

At the Atlantic City Convention in August, a compromise was offered: Only two MFDP members would be seated as at-large delegates. Moses's group rejected the compromise and staged a sit-in on the convention floor before walking out.

Moses was gaining a following that he did not want. He had no wish to be a leader, he just wanted to organize. He began going by the name Robert Parris and soon after, in 1966, he left SNCC and the movement for private life. He taught in Africa for a while, then returned to the United States in 1976 and won a MacArthur Fellowship in 1980.

ELIJAH MUHAMMAD

For 41 years, Elijah Muhammad, the controversial head of the Nation of Islam, was the leading proponent in spreading the Islamic religion throughout Black America. He was instrumental in creating a self-help movement through which many African Americans could determine and control their own destinies.

Born Elijah Poole in Sandersville, Georgia, on October 10, 1897, Muhammad was one of 13 children of former slaves. A major turning point in his life came when Poole, as a child, secretly witnessed the lynching of a Black man by three Whites.

This traumatic event may have led to Muhammad's ultimate belief that Blacks and Whites should live apart, independently. He spurred the Nation of Islam movement into the direction of a separatist entity.

Poole moved to Detroit in 1923. In the 1930s, he became a follower of Wallace Fard, who preached that by practicing their "original" religion, Islam, Blacks could overcome their conditions of degradation in America.

Fard encouraged Poole to reject his "slave" name and adopt an Islamic one; Poole became Elijah Muhammad. Fard then appointed Muhammad as supreme minister of the Nation of Islam, also known as the Black Muslims. When Fard disappeared in 1934, Muhammad preached that Fard had actually been Allah in disguise, who shared secrets and teachings with Muhammad. This made Muhammad "The Messenger of Allah." Muhammad began traveling the country, spreading the teachings of the Muslim movement.

Arrested in 1934 for not sending his children to a public school (they attended a Nation of Islam school), Muhammad lived as a fugitive from 1934 to 1942. In 1942, he was jailed for three years for resisting the draft. After his release in 1946, he continued his influential reign as head of the Nation of Islam. About four years later, Muhammad recruited Malcolm X to be the national spokesman for the Muslims. The 13 years Malcolm X spent in that position were the organization's most fruitful (prior to Minister Louis Farrakhan's rise to power).

Muhammad and the Black Muslims earned growing respect because of their comportment. They were self-respecting, highly moral individuals who did not smoke, drink, gamble, or take drugs. Self-disciplined and courteous, they maintained intact family units.

Muhammad used his followers to show that every Black person has the potential to reach the same level of dignity, with no assistance from White America. To support his ideology of separatism, Muhammad had his organization create and develop their own alternative institutions.

By the time of his death on February 25, 1975, from congestive heart failure brought on by lifelong bronchial problems, Muhammad's Nation of Islam controlled a vast empire estimated at $80 to $100 million. The group's holdings included schools, a university, numerous farms and small businesses, a publishing company, an airplane, an import business, orchards, dairies, refrigerator trucks, apartment complexes, several mansions, and hundreds of houses of worship.

Left: *One of Muhammad's strongest desires was the creation of an independent Black nation located on land in the southern portion of the country, which he wanted ceded to the Nation of Islam by the United States government.* Right: *A Black Muslim member displays a copy of the Nation of Islam's* Muhammad Speaks *newspaper.*

ISAAC MURPHY

ISAAC MURPHY,
ONE OF THE GREATEST JOCKEYS OF
ALL TIME, WAS THE FIRST TO WIN
THREE KENTUCKY DERBYS, A FEAT
UNSURPASSED FOR 57 YEARS. HE
WON 44 PERCENT OF ALL HIS
RACES AND AT ONE POINT HAD A
STREAK OF 49 WINS OUT OF
51 RACES.

Little Isaac Murphy was the closest thing to perfection that any jockey has ever been—he set amazing records that in most respects have not been topped.

Named Isaac Burns, he was a slave born in Lexington, Kentucky, possibly on January 1 (the birth date given for all Thoroughbred horses), in 1866. His father died in the Civil War as a Union soldier. After the Emancipation Proclamation, his family moved to the Lexington farm of his mother's father, Green Murphy. Isaac took his grandfather's surname.

The story goes that at the age of 12, the family added two years to Murphy's age so that he could get an apprentice jockey's license. Murphy ran his first race in Louisville in May 1875, but didn't win a meet until 16 months later. That win began an unparalleled string of successes.

Murphy became the first jockey to win the Kentucky Derby three times—1884, 1890, 1891—and the first to win back-to-back Derbys. He also won four of the first five runnings of the American Derby at Washington Park in Chicago (1884 to 1886, and 1888). In 1882, at Saratoga Downs in New York, he ran an incredible string of 49 victories in 51 starts.

Murphy's three Kentucky Derby wins went unmatched for 39 years, when Earl Sande tied the mark in 1930. The record also went unsurpassed for 57 years, until Eddie Arcaro won his fourth of five Derbys in 1948.

For his career, Murphy won 628 races out of a total 1,412 mounts—an astonishing 44 percent clip. It's little wonder that he was the first rider voted into the Jockey Hall of Fame, in 1955.

Track aficionados suggest that Murphy knew how to pace a horse better than anyone the sport of racing had ever seen. It was said that he rode only with his hands and heels and only used the whip to satisfy the crowd. Like most of the young riders of his day, Murphy virtually lived and slept at the track. He became proficient at the art of hand-riding, which made the rider more in tune with his mount. Legend had it that a horse could jump straight up and down, but Murphy would never raise off his back. He seemed to be part of the horse. Newspapers and trainers of the day called him the greatest jockey.

Murphy was also noted for his integrity, honesty, honor, and character. He was the undisputed king of his profession, which had the largest spectator attendance of any sport in America at the time.

By 1882, his salary was $10,000 a year. It is estimated that Murphy earned more than

$250,000 in his career—an amazing sum of money in those days.

Murphy was the head-to-head winner of one of the most publicized races of the late 19th century. To settle a debate whether he could beat the best White jockey of the day, Snapper Garrison, Murphy emerged from the race victorious.

Ironically, Murphy almost didn't participate in his first Kentucky Derby victory. The horse he was to ride, Buchanan, had almost thrown him in a race only a few weeks before and Murphy wanted nothing more to do with the animal. The horse's owner threatened to suspend him, so Murphy rode Buchanan in the Derby, and won.

Unfortunately, Murphy's career virtually ended following his third Derby victory in 1891. He was prone to putting on weight during the off-season and would balloon up to 140 pounds or more over the winter. Then he would diet before the spring races.

This unhealthy practice eventually weakened his body and made him prone to infection. He caught pneumonia and died on February 12, 1896, at the age of 35.

Murphy was considered the best of the Black jockeys. In the first Kentucky Derby in 1875, 14 of the 15 riders were Black.

In fact, from 1875 to 1911, 11 Black jockeys won 15 Kentucky Derbys and many other major races throughout the South. The Black jockeys rode so well, however, that their White peers arranged for their ejection from the sport. They created a governing body that refused to relicense the Black jockeys. There has been almost no participation in the sport of horse racing by Black riders since, despite the acclaim Murphy received throughout America in his heyday.

Murphy was the best jockey in America at a time when horse racing was America's premier spectator sport. Popular in the late 1800s, Black jockeys were segregated from racing around the turn of the century and have had almost no impact on the sport to this day.

Track-and-field specialist James Cleveland "Jesse" Owens ran like the wind—legend had it that he'd be across the finish line before you could see him take off. His speed led to one of America's proudest moments on the world stage.

Owens was born September 12, 1913, and his father was an illiterate Alabama field laborer. His gift came to light early when he consistently outran the local boys, though the frail lad suffered from malnutrition.

An amazed and sympathetic coach, Charles Riley, took Owens under his wing. Riley worked him out for 45 minutes a day before school, while Owens worked several jobs after classes. Riley's efforts paid off: As a high school senior, Owens tied the world record in the 100-yard dash and won three events in the 1933 National Interscholastic Championships in Chicago. It was the first of several astonishing track meets that would put Owens in the record books.

The next came on May 25, 1935, when, as an Ohio State University student, Owens participated in a Big Ten Conference track meet at the University of Michigan. The 21-year-old tied the world record for the 100-yard dash and set new world records for the 220-yard dash, the 220-yard low hurdles, and the broad jump (as the long jump was called at that time).

His crowning moment was to come. At the 1936 Olympic Games in Berlin, Germany, Owens won four gold medals and, before the eyes of the world, dashed Adolf Hitler's boasts of Aryan superiority. Not only did Owens win the gold, but he tied the Olympic record for the 100-meter dash and set new Olympic records for the 200-meter run and the long jump.

The coup de grâce came when Owens ran the final leg of the 400-meter relay race, in which the American team broke a world

JESSE OWENS WON FOUR GOLD MEDALS FOR AMERICA IN THE 1936 OLYMPIC GAMES IN BERLIN, GERMANY, WHICH EMBARRASSED ADOLF HITLER WORLDWIDE. HIS LONG JUMP RECORD STOOD FOR 25 YEARS AND FOR A TIME OWENS HELD OR SHARED THE WORLD RECORD FOR EVERY SPRINT EVENT RECOGNIZED BY THE INTERNATIONAL AMATEUR ATHLETIC FEDERATION.

record. Hitler was so disgusted that he refused to shake Owens's hand, though he had personally congratulated other earlier Olympic winners.

Unfortunately, though Owens was celebrated on his return to America, he was not embraced. Promised endorsements never materialized. Penniless, he hired himself out to race against horses and motorcycles. He couldn't afford to finish college and finally landed a job as a city playground worker.

It wasn't until 1955 that America began to recognize Owens's accomplishments. The government sent him abroad as an Ambassador of Sports and he gave speeches on patriotism and fair play. He was also named secretary of the Illinois State Athletic Commission.

Following his death on March 31, 1980, in Arizona, Jesse Owens was posthumously awarded the Congressional Medal of Honor in 1990 and also appeared on a commemorative postage stamp.

Facing page: Owens's record-setting career started early; he tied the world record in the 100-yard dash as a senior in high school. Left: Owens (far left) with the winning 400-meter relay team that embarrassed Hitler in the 1936 Olympics.

She was born Rosa Louise McCauley in Tuskegee, Alabama, in 1913. For the next 42 years, she would live her life in obscurity until one fateful day in Montgomery, Alabama. Then everything would change.

Three weeks before Christmas in 1955, in Montgomery, 42-year-old seamstress Rosa Parks joined the tired workers at the bus stop after a hard day at her tailoring job. It seemed like the bus would never come. When it finally arrived, all the seats in the back, where Blacks were allowed to sit, were quickly taken. Parks sat down in the White section. The bus driver told her and several other African Americans to give up their seats to Whites. Parks refused to move. The bus driver called the police and Parks was arrested. She and her husband later lost their jobs.

Her refusal to give up her seat sparked a movement against segregation in Montgomery, which started with a 381-day bus boycott by African Americans. The leader of that boycott went on to become quite famous—a young Black minister named Dr. Martin Luther King, Jr. He used his church to organize the boycott. So successful was the boycott that Dr. King was arrested and his life was threatened. Subsequently, King and his father, Martin Luther King, Sr., and other ministers, including the reverends Ralph Abernathy and Wyatt T. Walker, founded the Southern Christian Leadership Conference (SCLC). These events, kicked off by Parks's nonviolent passive resistance, officially launched the Civil Rights Movement. On December 21, 1956, the boycott ended, with the U.S. Supreme Court declaring bus segregation unconstitutional.

This was not Parks's first attempt to fight discrimination. In the 1930s, Parks and her husband, Raymond, had worked courageously in a futile attempt to free the Scottsboro Boys, nine Black men who were falsely accused of raping two White women. "To do anything open for this cause, could be death," she said. In 1944, Parks had also refused to go to the back of the bus and had been forced to get off. During the 1950s, Parks was the secretary of the Montgomery branch of the NAACP.

ROSA PARKS'S REFUSAL TO SUBMIT TO WHITE PRIVILEGE KICKED OFF A LIBERATION STRUGGLE THAT NAMED HER THE "MOTHER OF THE CIVIL RIGHTS MOVEMENT."

These incidents changed Parks's life. Later, she and her husband moved to Detroit, where she still lives. For more than 23 years, she served as a staff assistant to Representative John Conyers of Michigan. In 1994, Parks, then 81 years old, was attacked by a robber. After community help, the robber was caught, convicted, and he apologized.

In the mid-1990s, Parks wrote her first autobiography, *Rosa Parks: My Story*, then authored *Quiet Strength*, an autobiography with Gregory Reed, which focuses on the faith, hope, and heart of a woman who changed a nation by starting the Civil Rights Movement. In her book, Parks recalls her outrage as a Black woman at being asked to stand up so a White man could sit down.

"After so many years of oppression and being a victim of mistreatment that my people had suffered, not giving up my seat—and whatever I had to face after not giving it up—was not important."

Facing page: *For more than 40 years, Rosa Parks has been a guiding symbol in the struggle for Black equality.* Left: *Parks, accompanied by E. D. Nixon, former president of the Alabama NAACP, arrives at the Montgomery, Alabama, courthouse on March 19, 1956. She stood trial for refusing to yield her bus seat to a White man.*

SIDNEY POITIER

At one brief point in his life, Sidney Poitier was a homeless teenager sleeping on Harlem rooftops. But he became a significant film star and the first Black actor to make it big in dramatic movies. He often had the leading role in these serious nonstereotypical movies.

Despite a formal education of less than two years, Poitier polished himself to the point that he won the Best Actor Oscar in 1963 for his touching performance as a handyman who helped a group of nuns build a chapel in *Lilies of the Field.* He was the first African-American actor to win the award in that category and helped change the stereotype of Blacks presented in movies.

Poitier was born February 20, 1927, in Miami, the seventh child of West Indian parents, who raised him in the Bahamas. Because of their poverty, Poitier returned to Miami to live with an older brother. He drifted to New York with only a small amount of money and the clothes on his back. He survived by working various jobs, mostly dish-washing, until he lied about his age in order to join the Army.

After being discharged in 1945, Poitier returned to New York and auditioned for the American Negro Theater (ANT), which rejected him because of his thick Caribbean accent and poor reading skills. Undaunted, Poitier listened to the radio for six months to learn how to speak without an accent and had a friend tutor him in reading. When he applied to the ANT again, in 1946, he was accepted and began to work.

Poitier played in the Black Broadway production of *Lysistrata* and the Broadway and touring productions of *Anna Lucasta* in 1948. He made an Army training film in 1949. In 1950, he received his first Hollywood role in *No Way Out.* In the mid-1950s, roles in *Blackboard Jungle, Edge of the City,* and *The Defiant Ones* (for which he received his first Best Actor nomination) established Poitier as a box office draw.

Those roles also created a character that would become a Poitier trademark through-

out his career—a sincere, sometimes angry, but generally good-hearted, highly moral, intelligent Black man of great dignity. This was typified by his role in 1967's *Guess Who's Coming to Dinner,* a story of interracial romance.

The biggest exception to that image was Poitier's brilliant portrayal of Walter Lee Younger in the play and movie versions of *A Raisin in the Sun,* as a profoundly flawed Black man distraught by the limitations placed on his life because of his race.

Poitier found additional success in the 1970s directing and starring in the Black western *Buck and the Preacher* and several comedies with Bill Cosby and other African-American stars. He also directed Richard Pryor and Gene Wilder in *Stir Crazy* in 1980, which grossed $58 million.

In 1992, the American Film Institute awarded Poitier the Life Achievement Award, the Institute's highest honor.

Left: *Poitier meets the press after receiving his Best Actor award for his performance in* Lilies of the Field.
Right: *Poitier's stage debut was in the American Theatre in* Days of Our Lives. *He was the understudy and when the star, Harry Belafonte, could not go on, Poitier played the starring role.*

ADAM CLAYTON POWELL, JR.

NEW YORK CONGRESSMAN

ADAM CLAYTON POWELL, JR., WAS

ONE OF THE FIRST AND LOUDEST

VOICES IN WHAT WAS TO BECOME

THE CIVIL RIGHTS MOVEMENT.

ONLY THE FOURTH BLACK

REPRESENTATIVE ELECTED IN THE

20TH CENTURY, THE FLAMBOYANT,

IMMENSELY POPULAR POWELL

FOUGHT TO END HIRING

DISCRIMINATION AND

SEGREGATION IN PUBLIC

FACILITIES.

Ten years before the Civil Rights Movement became full-fledged, New York Congressman Adam Clayton Powell, Jr., was a singular strong voice in government advocating the abolition of segregation and employment discrimination.

When Powell went to the House of Representatives in 1945, he became the first Black congressman from the northeastern United States and only the fourth Black representative in the 20th century. Powell agitated for immediate, total equality of the races. More conservative Black leaders of his day were arguing for more gradual change.

From the beginning, Powell pushed legislation to desegregate the military and public transportation, make lynching a federal crime, recruit Black nurses into the armed forces, establish a permanent Fair Employment Practices Commission, and deny federal funds to public schools practicing discrimination.

Powell also took his congressional colleagues to task for their racist attitudes, confronting them when they used the word "nigger" on the House floor, and deriding segregationist members—one even punched him during a session.

His brand of uncompromising, defiant agitation endeared Powell to his Harlem con-

stituency, which by large margins reelected him to Congress for 25 years.

Powell was born on November 29, 1908, in New Haven, Connecticut, but came to New York when his father was offered the pastorship of the Abyssinian Baptist Church in Harlem. Though Powell became a notorious socializer, a trait that compromised his political effectiveness, he promised his parents he would enter the ministry.

Powell graduated from Colgate University in 1930, then received his master's degree in religion from Columbia University in 1932. He took over Abyssinian when his father retired in 1937. Powell used his pulpit to address a variety of political and social issues, particularly employment discrimination. He also wrote political pieces for the *New York Post* and was a popular columnist in Harlem's *Amsterdam* newspaper.

In 1941, Powell was elected to New York's City Council, then, in 1944, decided to take his fight national by running for Congress and winning. By 1961, his seniority put Powell in line to chair the powerful House Committee on Education and Labor. In five years, he passed 49 major laws from the committee.

However, Powell's brash nature, flamboyant lifestyle, and controversy about his finances caused his colleagues to strip Powell of his chairmanship and expel him from his congressional seat in 1967. Ironically, he won a special election to fill his own vacancy and the Supreme Court declared Congress's actions against him unconstitutional. But Powell only occasionally showed up in Congress afterward.

He went into seclusion on the Caribbean island of Bimini and died in Miami on April 4, 1972.

Facing page: *During a 1966 press conference, Powell called for $7 billion to fund the federal Anti-Poverty Program, more than four times the amount requested by the administration of President Lyndon Johnson.* Below: *Powell arrives at his 1960 trial on income tax evasion in a car owned by the New York church that he pastored. The jury deadlocked on the charges and Powell was not tried again.*

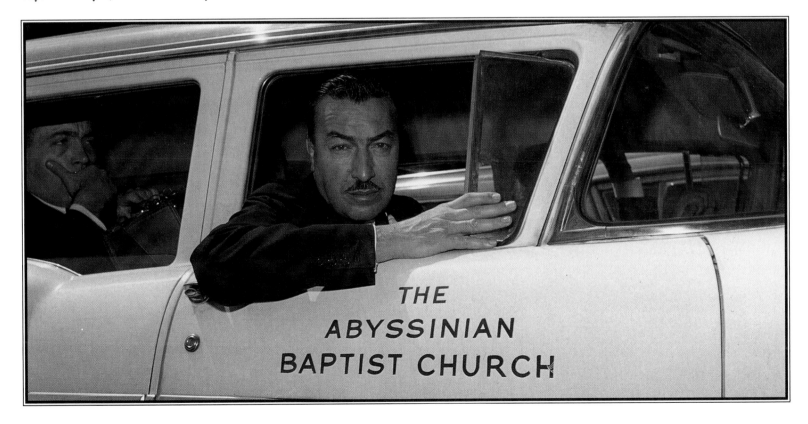

THE ABYSSINIAN BAPTIST CHURCH

COLIN POWELL

It has only been about 50 years between the segregation of World War II and the present, when an African American has risen to one of the highest military posts possible—Chairman of the Joint Chiefs of Staff.

Colin Powell was born April 5, 1937, near the end of the Depression in Harlem. His father was foreman in the shipping department for a garment district firm and his mother was a seamstress. Powell first went to P.S. 39 elementary school and then to Morris High School in the Bronx, like most of the other neighborhood teens. From there he went to City College where he grew to like the discipline of ROTC, the Reserve Officers Training Corps, where young men trained for the military. Powell also worked six years part-time at a neighborhood baby furniture store called Sicksers, owned by Lou Kirschner's father-in-law. It was at this store where Powell picked up Yiddish from Kirschner—a linguistic facility that would later earn him the moniker of "Black Jew" during his early Pentagon years.

In ROTC's "Pershing Rifles" fraternity at City College, Powell adapted well to the structure and discipline in school. After graduating from college as a newly commissioned second lieutenant, he went to training in the South. After a few years there, he married the Birmingham beauty Alma Johnson, then he went to Vietnam.

Biographer Howard Means said in *Colin Powell* that Powell was leading a combat unit near the North Vietnamese border when his son was born. A few weeks later, on a patrol near the Laotian border, he was wounded when he stepped into a booby-trap rigged with a sharpened punji stick that drove all the way through his left foot. He received a Purple Heart.

Powell's career began to take off in the late 1960s after he enrolled in the prestigious U.S. Army's Command and General Staff College. A decade later, he was a brigadier general. He took several high echelon military courses as well as receiving a master's degree from George Washington University.

THIS YIDDISH-SPEAKING,
HARLEM-BORN SON OF JAMAICAN IMMIGRANTS ROSE ABOVE ALMOST INSURMOUNTABLE OBSTACLES TO BECOME THE FIRST AFRICAN-AMERICAN CHAIRMAN OF THE JOINT CHIEFS OF STAFF AND A BEST-SELLING AUTHOR.

After that, a succession of Pentagon jobs started coming his way.

He came to the attention of America when he became the first Black National Security Advisor under President Reagan in 1987. Powell moved up to become the Chairman of the Joint Chiefs of Staff under President Bush, just in time for Operation Desert Storm in Kuwait. Powell emerged from Desert Storm as a real American hero.

In 1995, with the release of his best-selling autobiography, Powell flirted with the possibility of running for president. He ultimately decided the time was not right for him and his family, though polls said he was a strong candidate.

Left: *Powell conducted regular White House news briefings during Operation Desert Storm and on other matters of national security.* Right: *During a Memorial Day celebration in 1991, the general greets Corporal Patrick McElrath, who was wounded in the U.S. invasion of Panama in 1989.*

A. PHILIP RANDOLPH

Asa Philip Randolph fought a lifelong battle to provide fair employment opportunities for African Americans. His work as a trade unionist and organizer directly resulted in the establishment of the first successful Black labor union, desegregation of the armed forces, and the end of employment discrimination by companies and government bureaus involved in the defense industry.

Randolph pioneered the use of mass, nonviolent, direction action protests to win gains from the federal government that benefited African Americans. His methods were replicated in the Civil Rights Movement, of which Randolph served as senior statesman.

He was born April 15, 1889, in Crescent City, Florida, to modest middle-class parents. Randolph moved to New York City in 1911 after being unable to find decent work in his native Florida. That experience had an indelible effect on him—the beginning of his struggle to secure the rights of the Black working class.

Almost immediately, Randolph became involved in union efforts and Socialist politics in New York. He also attended the City College of New York, taking classes in political science, economics, philosophy, and history. In 1912, he founded an employment agency and attempted to organize Black workers.

In 1917, following the entry of America into World War I, Randolph and friend Chandler Owen founded *The Messenger* magazine (later called *The Black Worker*), which called for increased hiring in the war industry and armed forces for African Americans.

Randolph helped to organize the Socialist Party's first all-Black political club in New York City. Eventually, he relinquished his formal ties to the party, but he continued to consider himself a Democratic socialist.

His growing reputation as a labor organizer brought Randolph to the attention of the Black porters, who took care of passengers on Pullman sleeping car trains. Being a Pullman porter was a plum job for Blacks, but the porters were still besieged with poor working conditions, including low pay and long hours.

LABOR ORGANIZER

A. PHILIP RANDOLPH ESTABLISHED THE FIRST SUCCESSFUL BLACK TRADE UNION AND WAS RESPONSIBLE FOR THE DESEGREGATION OF THE ARMED FORCES AND DEFENSE INDUSTRIES. HE WAS ALSO THE PREDOMINANT BLACK LEADER BETWEEN THE ERAS OF BOOKER T. WASHINGTON AND MARTIN LUTHER KING, JR.

In 1925, Randolph was hired as an organizer and founded the Brotherhood of Sleeping Car Porters. The Pullman Company had crushed earlier efforts by the porters to organize. Randolph fought the Pullman Company for 12 years, but in 1937, the company signed a major labor contract with the Brotherhood. Randolph had forged the first successful Black trade union, which he took into the American Federation of Labor (AFL), despite the discrimination in its own ranks.

Randolph's success with Pullman launched his ascension as a national Black leader. Following the certification of the Brotherhood as a bargaining agent, Randolph returned to his fight for Black inclusion in the military and the defense industry. He threatened to lead a massive march on Washington, D.C., in 1941, and bring an invasion of thousands of Blacks to the White House lawn.

Left: *Randolph was an unceasing agitator for the rights of the Black working class. His work helped integrate the military and labor unions.* Right: *Randolph stands in front of a model of a Pullman car named after him. He successfully waged a battle, which was 12 years long, with the Pullman Company to get a labor contract for the Pullman porters.*

Above: *Randolph poses with a group of women at the Black Heritage Museum in Pittsburgh in 1952.*

executive order in 1948 to ban segregation in the military. Though Randolph didn't follow through with either threat, the results revealed the power of mass demonstrations.

Randolph spent the 1950s pursuing civil rights activities, particularly in the field of labor. After the AFL merged with the Congress of Industrial Organizations (CIO) in 1955, Randolph became the only Black member of the Executive Council. He used that platform to establish the Negro American Labor Council to attack segregation within the AFL-CIO.

The culmination of his career came when Randolph, at the age of 74, served as director and chairman of the 1963 March on Washington, D.C., for Jobs and Freedom. The next year, President Lyndon Johnson presented him with the Presidential Medal of Freedom, the nation's highest civilian honor.

He remained involved in his activities as a vice president of the AFL-CIO until 1968, focusing on ending discrimination in unions. His criticism of the union often landed him in hot water with union brass. By the end of his labor career, Randolph's agitation had made the AFL-CIO one of the most integrated public institutions in America.

He died May 16, 1979, in New York City at the age of 90.

Seeing that Randolph was successfully mobilizing the forces needed to make the march a reality, President Franklin Roosevelt issued an executive order banning discrimination by companies with defense contracts. This was the federal government's first commitment to fair employment practices.

The success of that effort gave Randolph leverage to lay down another threat. He proposed that Blacks boycott the draft. The potential of this confrontation may have influenced President Harry Truman to issue an

Coretta Scott King greets Randolph at an 80th birthday tribute held in his honor in New York City. Many public officials and labor leaders were present to celebrate his birthday and his many accomplishments.

PAUL ROBESON

Athlete, actor, activist, academician, orator, singer, lawyer, linguist, Paul Robeson was a true "Renaissance man." He was so gifted that he was celebrated throughout the world.

Robeson was born April 9, 1898, in Princeton, New Jersey, the son of a former slave minister father and school teacher mother, who died when Paul was six. After graduating high school with honors in 1915, he won an academic scholarship to prestigious Rutgers University. Though the only Black student there, he was extremely popular.

Robeson received national attention for his athletic abilities at Rutgers. As an all-around athlete, he earned 12 varsity letters in football, track, baseball, and basketball; he was twice named football All-American.

He excelled just as well with his studies. Robeson won Rutgers' major oratorical contests four years in a row, and he earned Phi Beta Kappa (the nation's highest scholastic honor) in his junior year. In 1919, Robeson graduated as valedictorian of his class.

Deciding not to become a full-time professional athlete, Robeson entered Columbia University to obtain his law degree, which he did in 1923. He played pro football on weekends to support himself and his wife, Eslanda. She was a fellow Columbia student and chemist who was the first African American to work at New York's Presbyterian Hospital.

After graduation, Robeson briefly worked at a prestigious law firm. He soon quit because of the lack of opportunity for Blacks in the legal profession at the time and because of discriminatory practices.

Robeson drifted into stage acting, having appeared in amateur productions in college. He met dramatist Eugene O'Neill in 1924 and quickly signed as lead in O'Neill's *All God's Chillun Got Wings* and *The Emperor Jones*.

Robeson's booming baritone and acting skills garnered instant acclaim.

Beginning in 1925, he sang immensely successful concerts of gospel spirituals and folk songs across the country. In 1927, Robeson opened in London in the musical *Show Boat* and sang "Ol' Man River." That song has become an American classic forever associated with Robeson's deep tones.

With his star steadily rising, Robeson continued giving concerts to capacity crowds and starring in plays such as *John Henry* and *The Hairy Ape*. In 1943, when he starred as Othello with an all-White cast, the production set a record for the longest Broadway run of a Shakespearean play. Some consider it one of the most memorable events in the history of the theater. He also performed the play in London to acclaim.

By 1945, Robeson had become the most famous Black man in America. He appeared in a dozen movies, including *King Solomon's Mines*, *Proud Valley*, *Sanders of the River*, *The Song of Freedom,* and the film versions of *Show Boat* and *The Emperor Jones*. In most of these movies, Robeson played Black characters with dignity, in contrast to the stereotype African-American roles of Hollywood films of that day.

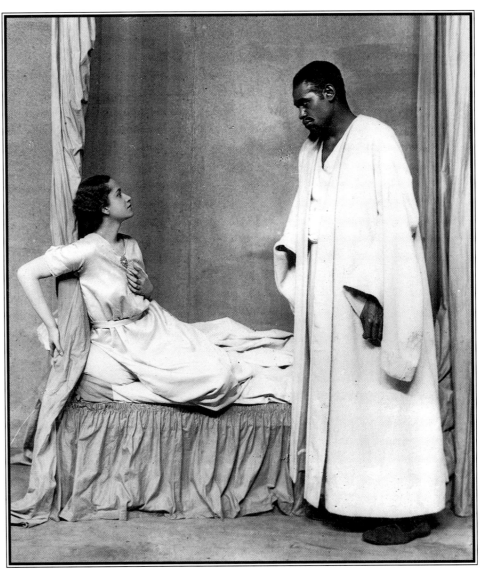

Facing page: *A young Robeson arrives back in the United States to visit his wife, who was ill. He had been in a play in London and was the leading man in the production.* Above: *Robeson plays Othello, opposite Peggy Ashcroft, in London in 1930. His performance thrilled audiences, and he played to vast critical acclaim.*

Robeson on the set of Show Boat, *the 1936 film. His rendition of "Ol' Man River" is still the best known song from the movie.*

Robeson was a staunch opponent of racism and spent much of his time and energy fighting for equality for Blacks in America. His frequent international concert tours colored his world view. He learned more than 20 languages, including Russian, and began to study his African heritage and its culture. Robeson and his family visited the Soviet Union in 1934. After being received warmly, they decided to remain for several years.

Robeson became a supporter of progressive causes around the globe, including the rights of oppressed Jews, of anti-Fascist forces in Spain, and of African nations against European colonial powers. The more he studied ideas of universal fellowship and world peace, the more he spoke out here and abroad on the plight of Blacks in America.

Robeson met with President Harry Truman to urge him to do something about the lynchings of Blacks in the South. His increasingly vocal opposition drew the ire of some people, who labeled him "un-American."

As the Cold War with the Soviet Union heated up, in 1950 the State Department withdrew Robeson's passport because of alleged communist affiliations. Robeson vowed that he had never been a member of the Communist Party, but would not sign an oath disavowing communism. This brought the great entertainer's singing and acting career to an end. Both Blacks and Whites in America turned their backs on him. He was not allowed to travel abroad for eight years. The Supreme Court restored his passport in 1958 after declaring the oath he was asked to sign unconstitutional.

With his passport restored, Robeson left the country and toured until 1963. Ill health forced him back to America and retirement. Robeson, 77, died January 23, 1976.

Robeson in costume for the 1933 film The Emperor Jones. *Robeson soon left the show business spotlight to enter into human rights activism. In 1934, he visited the Soviet Union. He and his family were warmly received and they decided to live there for some time. His continued activism eventually led to the State Department's withdrawing his passport, though the Supreme Court restored it in 1958.*

JACKIE ROBINSON

JACKIE ROBINSON

WILL LONG BE REMEMBERED AS THE FIRST BLACK MAJOR-LEAGUE BASEBALL PLAYER AND THE FIRST AFRICAN AMERICAN ELECTED TO THE BASEBALL HALL OF FAME.

Jack Roosevelt Robinson was born in Cairo, Georgia, in 1919, when many cities were erupting in race riots. World War I Black soldiers were returning from segregated quarters in the military to increased discrimination at home.

Two decades later, Robinson, a top UCLA athlete, became the school's first four-letter man. He excelled in basketball, football, track, and baseball.

A year later, World War II was starting and Robinson, swept up in the fervor, entered the army as a draftee applying for Officer Candidate School (OCS). He was turned down because he was Black. Robinson, not one to take no for an answer, consulted with his friend and fellow draftee, World Heavyweight Champion Joe Louis. Louis used his clout to get Robinson accepted in OCS. Robinson became a second lieutenant who spent the rest of the war fighting segregation at bases in Kansas and Texas instead of fighting enemies in Germany and Japan.

It was during this tumultuous time that Robinson became friends with Branch Rickey, president of the Brooklyn Dodgers. Rickey encouraged the young athlete to use his talents and energies integrating major-league baseball. According to Rickey, Robinson could help him take a losing team to the winner's circle while breaking the "color line."

Rickey hated segregation as much as Robinson. Rickey had once seen a Black college player turned away from a hotel. He got the player a cot in his room. Rickey never forgot seeing this player crying because he was denied a place to lay his weary head just because of the color of his skin. Rickey wanted to change things. He saw a way to do just that with the talented, poised Jackie Robinson.

Robinson played shortstop with the Negro League Kansas City Monarchs, never losing sight of his ultimate dream, to play with Rickey's Brooklyn Dodgers. Finally, Rickey's scouts caught up with Robinson and invited him to come to New York. Told of the immense difficulties he would have if he played with an all-White team, the ever-confident Robinson agreed anyway. He gave his word there would never be an incident and he kept it despite a lifetime of standing up to bigotry. Robinson had to endure fans calling him ugly names. Players, even sports writers, defamed him with comments about being the first Black to play on an all-White team. But Robinson didn't fight back. He knew his actions could ruin the chances of other African-American players. Besides, he gave Branch Rickey his word.

After a year at the Dodgers' top farm team, the Montreal Royals, Robinson displayed amazing skill, winning the hearts of many who saw this Black wizard play ball. In his very first game, he hit a three-run homer. That year, the team won the Little World Series. At Robinson's last game in Montreal, the crowd stormed the field, recited Robinson's name repeatedly, hoisted him on their shoulders, and paraded him around the field.

By 1947, after officially joining the Dodgers, Robinson was named Rookie of the Year by *Sporting News* magazine. He helped the Dodgers win a National League pennant. Ford Frick, who was president of the National League, gave Robinson a Silver Bat award for winning the National League batting title. Robinson also led the league in stolen bases and hit .297. This was the beginning of a series of accolades he would garner in his brilliant 10-year career with the team.

In 1949, the same year he captured the National League Most Valuable Player Award, two former teammates from the Negro

Facing page: Robinson, a student at UCLA, performs his heroics in a track event. He was the school's first four-letter man. Above: Robinson at bat in 1950. His swing could strike fear into the heart of any major-league pitcher.

Above: *Robinson gets caught off base, a rare event for the adept base stealer.* Facing page: *Robinson's all-around skills earned him election into the Baseball Hall of Fame in 1962, the first year he was eligible.*

leagues joined him on the All-Star Team—Roy Campanella and Don Newcombe. Robinson was still receiving threats on his life for playing a "White man's game," despite his great success. Robinson responded to a hate letter by hitting a home run in the next game he played.

In 1955, the Dodgers won the World Series—a feat that Robinson called "one of the greatest thrills in my life." In 1957, at age 39, he retired with a lifetime batting average of .311. And by 1962, Robinson became the first African American elected to Baseball's Hall of Fame.

Robinson went on to become both a civil rights activist and businessman. On the business end, he became vice president of a company called Chock Full O'Nuts. Now that other Blacks had joined him in integrating baseball, he was free to actively fight discrimination. His activism caught the attention of Martin Luther King, Jr., and Jesse Jackson, both of whom consulted with him on a variety of social justice issues. Additionally, Robinson continued to be a staunch supporter of the NAACP. Robinson's quest for economic justice for African-American entrepreneurs inspired him to reestablish the Freedom National Bank in Harlem in 1964, which was owned and operated by Blacks.

Early in 1972, the Dodgers retired Robinson's number 42. Robinson died of a heart attack on October 24, 1972, in his Stamford, Connecticut, home just a few days after he threw out the first pitch at the 1972 World Series. The Reverend Jesse Jackson eulogized the trailblazing athlete at the funeral. Robinson's ideas and values are kept alive today through the Jackie Robinson Foundation, a nonprofit organization launched in 1973 by Rachel Robinson, his widow. It provides leadership development and education for underprivileged youths.

JOHN RUSSWURM

TO SOME, HE WAS THE COFOUNDER OF THE BLACK PRESS. TO OTHERS, CRITICAL OF HIS EMIGRATION TO LIBERIA, HE WAS A TRAITOR. WHATEVER THE VIEW, SUPPORTERS AND CRITICS ALIKE ACKNOWLEDGE THAT JOHN BROWN RUSSWURM WAS AMERICA'S FIRST AFRICAN-AMERICAN NEWSPAPER EDITOR.

The premiere edition of the first Black newspaper *Freedom's Journal,* under the editorship of writer John Brown Russwurm and minister Samuel E. Cornish, hit the streets March 16, 1827. The place was New York City. Russwurm and Cornish became the fathers of the Black press and among the first champions of a free press, which then was a constitutional guarantee only for Whites.

"It is our earnest wish," they said in their maiden issue, "to make our *Freedom Journal* a medium of intercourse between our brethren in the different states of this great confederacy; that through its columns an expression of our sentiments, on many interesting subjects which concern us, may be offered to the public; that plans which are apparently beneficial may be candidly discussed and properly weighed. We wish to plead our cause. Too long have others spoken for us!"

Their controversial column took issue with the ambivalence of White liberals who said one thing and did another. It was because of the disenchantment Russwurm noticed in liberals and conservatives alike that he decided to pack his bags, turn his back on his White father, and go back to Africa where his West Indian mother's family was once kidnapped from.

Russwurm, who was also one of this country's first Black college graduates (Bowdoin), gave up his editorship and moved to Liberia. While living there, he edited the *Liberia Herald* and served as governor of the colony of Maryland, according to historian Lerone Bennett, Jr. He also worked for some time as the first superintendent for the schools. Russwurm moved to Liberia under the auspices of the American Colonization Society, a proslavery organization. Later, Russwurm and others distanced themselves from it, especially when abolitionists of both races were calling him a "Black traitor." Russwurm's critics contended that a mass exodus would strengthen the bonds of slavery by depriving slaves of support.

Disenchanted with the White male privilege in America, he said: "We consider it a waste of words to talk of ever enjoying citizenship in this country." Referring to the newly founded African republic of Liberia that he helped settle, Russwurm proudly said:

"This is our home and this is our country. Beneath its sod lies the bones of our fathers; for it some of them fought, bled, and died. Here we were born; and here we will die."

Like most of the back-to-Africa enthusiasts at the time, such as Paul Cuffee and Richard Allen, Russwurm was an artisan, an entrepreneur, and a pioneer of modest means. He sought to use his resources and talents to better the lot of the millions of American Blacks who were suffering under slavery. Russwurm and his colleagues were also very much influenced by the example of Touissant L'Ouverture and the Haitian revolutionaries. The equal rights philosophy, prudence, thrift, and sobriety maxims of Benjamin Franklin also motivated them. Russwurm's legacy lives on with the Black Press, which in 1996 celebrated its 169th year.

The National Newspaper Publisher's Association (NNPA), a national Black newspaper syndicate reaching 10 million African-American readers, gives the John Russwurm Trophy and Merit Award every year. They award the Merit Award, along with the John Russwurm Trophy, to a newspaper that "represents excellence in journalism," according to Bill Reed, managing director of the Washington-based NNPA.

Facing page: *John Russwurm was not only a pioneer of the Black press in America, but he also helped settle the African nation of Liberia, founded partially by repatriated African Americans.* Above: *Russwurm cofounded the United States's first Black newspaper,* Freedom's Journal, *along with minister Samuel E. Cornish (left). Cornish also edited* The Colored American, *circa 1837.*

DRED SCOTT

Dred Scott, a little man scarcely five-feet tall, was the principle in a case that many historians believe was one of the most significant events in American legal history.

Most schoolchildren know him as a man who sued his master for his freedom and took his case all the way to the Supreme Court. In 1857, Judge Roger Brook Taney gave the majority decision that Scott's removal to a free state did not make him free; that the state of Missouri determined Scott's status, which ruled that he was not free; and that Scott was not a citizen of Missouri, so could not sue in federal court against a citizen of another state. In essence, he ruled that constitutionally a Black man had "no rights that a White man was bound to respect."

During the 1830s and 1840s, Sam (he was later renamed Dred Scott) accompanied his master, a surgeon in the U.S. Army, on many trips to military posts around the country. These trips included visits to the free state of Illinois and the territory of Wisconsin. In 1846, Scott sued his master for his freedom, asserting his trips in slave-free areas made him free. A St. Louis paper described him as "illiterate but not ignorant" with "strong common sense."

Many northern states followed the doctrine of a famous English precedent, *Somerset* v. *Stewart*, which established the rule that a slave became free after setting foot in a free jurisdiction. After many delays, trials, and retrials, Scott's case reached the Supreme Court in 1856.

The court responded with nine separate opinions, and Chief Justice Taney delivered the majority opinion. Taney's ruling was consistent with one of his earlier rulings as Andrew Jackson's attorney general, which said that Black sailors on English vessels could be imprisoned in America when their ships docked. In other words, even foreign Blacks had no rights in this country.

Handed down by the Supreme Court in 1857, the Dred Scott ruling permitted slavery in the territories. Abraham Lincoln was dismayed. To him, the Dred Scott decision meant that slavery was again on the march and would possibly be forced upon the free states.

The decision outraged Black abolitionists and made them increasingly radical. It was also a spur to Black immigration attempts.

The ruling was both complex and controversial in that it unfolded against the background of several ominous developments—all of which underlined how Black people had lost ground in America. The first was that the Supreme Court overruled the Missouri Compromise of 1850 on the grounds that Congress did not have the authority to limit the expansion of slavery; slavery was found to be legal in the territories until the citizens voted for or against it. The second was that Africans and their descendants were found to be ineligible for citizenship in the United States as the framers of the Constitution had not viewed Africans as citizens at that time and they had not become citizens since.

Then there followed a second "final" settlement, the Kansas-Nebraska Act, which opened northern territory to settlement by slaveholders unless its settlers adopted an approved state constitution that prohibited it. The net effect of all this was the de facto nationalization of the slave system. The Dred Scott decision was the first instance in which major federal law was declared unconstitutional, and it was a landmark in the growth of judicial power.

Civil rights attorney Standish Willis described the legal impact of the Dred Scott decision this way: "Justice Taney based his harsh conclusion upon the pro-slavery clauses of the United States Constitution. He argued that under the Constitution slaves were property,

just like other property, and consequently, the Constitution permitted no distinction between types of property. In essence, slavery could not be abolished anywhere without first changing the U.S. Constitution."

Dred Scott fought his court battle for 12 years until Taney's Supreme Court decision went against him. He was 51 when the litigation was started on his behalf and 63 when he lost the case. Scott died from tuberculosis 18 months later on September 17, 1858.

For a few years before the Civil War, Dred Scott was the best known Black man in America. The Emancipation Proclamation of January 1, 1863, and the Thirteenth Amendment of the Constitution, adopted January 31, 1865, finally abolished slavery.

Scott actually won an early trial under Judge Alexander Hamilton in 1850, which granted him freedom because he had been taken to free states and territories. But the Missouri Supreme Court overturned Hamilton's ruling two years later and remanded Scott and his family back into slavery.

BESSIE SMITH

The turn of the century was a turning point for American culture; it marked the birth of two musicians who would create jazz and blues—Louis Armstrong and Bessie Smith. Two decades later, Armstrong would play on her hit recordings.

At the height of her brilliant career, the Harlem Renaissance was the rage. White critics began labeling blues and jazz recordings "race records," a not-so-subtle way to simultaneously disparage and market Black culture. Smith was earning about $2,000 a week—a phenomenal sum at that time. Before spell-bound audiences, the Empress of the Blues often groaned this song:

> I woke up this mornin'
> Can't even get out of my door
> I woke up this morning
> Can't even get out of my door
> That's enough trouble to make
> A poor girl wonder
> Where she wants to go

Musicians say Bessie Smith, a tall, heavyset woman, became a professional singer in her teens by being discovered by older blues singer Gertrude "Ma" Rainey. Rainey was so impressed with Smith that she hired her to be part of her Rabbit Foot Minstrel Troupe. Some say it was to teach her. Others say it was to prevent a younger and very talented Smith from rising up on Rainey's musical throne and taking over.

A record company scout spotted Smith during a minstrel performance in Philadelphia and immediately signed her to a recording contract. This led to Smith cutting 159 songs in the 1920s and early 1930s, including "Down-hearted Blues." Smith's phenomenal music was enhanced by her legendary producer, John Hammond, who would also discover her successor—Billie Holiday.

In tents, theaters, dance halls, cabarets, and juke joints and on records, Smith sang her blues. Writer Langston Hughes said that Smith's blues were the essence of "sadness . . . not softened with tears, but hardened with laughter." Other fans and critics were enchanted with the power and passion of her delivery. Her words were wellsprings of solace and hope. Like a spiritualist, she helped her patients cope with grief and disappointment. And like many healers, she internalized a lot of the pain.

Onstage, she was invincible, improbable, impregnable. Offstage, she tried to remain humble. This of course was her vulnerable side—a side with whom lovers and booze often found a familiar friend. Blues queens, like other African-American women in the 1920s, quested for independence. This search often manifested itself in the appearance of promiscuity, violence, and arrogance, partly because of the racial and sexual constraints society placed on women like Smith. She did not just sing the blues, she lived it. Her last appearance was at Harlem's Apollo Theater. Her fee had dropped to $250.

One could say it was racism and sexism that inspired Smith to fight for her life. One myth about her life says that racism took her

life. The official records report she died shortly after a huge truck pushed her off the road somewhere between Memphis and Huntsville, but Smith was possibly refused admittance to three all-White Mississippi hospitals. Whatever the truth may be, in 1937, singer Bessie Smith, the Empress of the Blues, hit that last note.

Facing page: Bessie Smith's performances were heartfelt—Smith didn't just sing the blues, she lived it. Left: At the height of her career in the 1920s, the Empress of the Blues was earning over $2,000 a week, truly a queenly sum. Smith inherited the position of First Lady of the Blues from the legendary "Ma" Rainey and turned it over to her successor, Billie Holiday.

MABEL STAUPERS

Often, little is said about Black women's struggle for equality. It was a long, hard fight before African-American women were allowed to participate in the military as nurses. In this campaign, one woman did make a difference: Mabel Staupers.

Staupers was born in 1890 in Barbados, British West Indies. She came to the United States with her family in 1903. She received her R.N. from Freedmen's Hospital in Washington, D.C., in 1917. Staupers became the superintendent of the Booker T. Washington Sanitorium, which was located in New York City, in 1920. She also served as a consultant on nursing to U.S. Surgeon-General James C. Magee in 1941, before she was elected president of the National Association of Colored Graduate Nurses (NACGN) in 1949.

The NACGN, led by Mabel Staupers, encouraged its members to enroll in the American Red Cross. At that time, the Red Cross was acting as a medical-staff procurement agency for the military, finding doctors and nurses to serve in the military. While the Red Cross said yes to Black women, the military said no.

In 1941, even after the attack on Pearl Harbor, both the Army and Navy Nurse Corps declared they would not accept Black nurses. The Army Nurse Corps later reluctantly reversed their Jim Crow policy after it was leaked to the press in 1941 that the Army Nurse Corps would accept 56 African-American nurses. These nurses were only to serve in segregated hospitals or wards, tending to only African-American soldiers, according to Staupers's biographer, Dr. Darlene Clark Hine, an expert on the plight of Black nurses.

Staupers's group was so outraged that they kicked off a huge media campaign to stop the American-style apartheid among military nurses. While their campaign publicly embarrassed a military that was being challenged on segregation on other fronts, two things occurred that helped the plight of Black nurses. First, White nurses went off to war, opening incredible opportunities at home. Also, the Cadet Nurse Corps was created to provide education grants to nurses, so many Black women were finally able to afford nursing school. By 1943, the army raised its quota of African-American nurses to 160.

Meanwhile, the handful of Black nurses that were allowed in the military were often subjected to harsh treatment. Black army nurses stationed in England, for example, were forced to attend to German prisoners of war. Only White nurses were allowed to treat the U.S. soldiers.

Staupers met with Eleanor Roosevelt in 1944 to protest the humiliation of Black army nurses. This is what she told the First Lady: "It is with high hopes that they [African-American nurses] will be used to nurse sick and wounded soldiers who are fighting our country's enemies and not primarily to care for these enemies." Her sharp words hit a chord with Mrs. Roosevelt. The restriction was eventually lifted.

Staupers published her autobiography in 1951 titled *No Time for Prejudice*. Because of her work, Staupers was awarded the prestigious NAACP Spingarn Medal in 1951 for her courageous efforts to integrate nurses into the military.

Staupers died of pneumonia October 1, 1989, at her home in Washington, D.C. She was 99 years old.

Staupers's voice was tireless in successfully calling for the entrance of Black nurses into the American military and then for equality of treatment for African-American nurses once they began to be recruited. Staupers even petitioned First Lady Eleanor Roosevelt in 1944 to protest the humiliation of Black Army nurses overseas. The nurses were not allowed to assist American soldiers; they could only treat enemy captives.

While much has been written about African-American musical contributions to jazz, blues, and rock, little has been penned about Black classical composers. The first African-American composer to have a symphonic work performed by a major American orchestra was Dr. William Grant Still. Called *Afro-American Symphony,* Still's stellar work premiered in 1931 with the Rochester Philharmonic under Dr. Howard Hanson. To this day, it remains a classic in its repertory. *Afro-American Symphony* has since been performed by other major orchestras throughout the world.

Additionally, Still's opera *Troubled Island,* based on a libretto by Langston Hughes, was the first African-American opera to be performed by a major company, the New York City Opera in 1949 under Laszlo Halasz in honor of the company's fifth anniversary. *Troubled Island* is based on the life of Haitian leader Jean-Jacques Dessalines, who ruled the world's first Black independent nation from 1804 to 1806. The libretto deals with the subject of Black liberation, and is above the usual operatic standard, in part because of Still's technical prowess and the passion of noted poet Hughes, who fashioned the work from a successful play. Reviewers for the New York *Herald Tribune* praised Still for having a flair for opera music, but punished him for not fully developing his ideas.

Still's work could be divided into three creative periods. The first was his experimental period (1920–1929), which some say was perhaps his most exciting period.

The second period (1930–1939), perhaps his most popular and prolific, was his African-American period when many of his works carried a Black theme. During this time he wrote "And They Lynched Him on a Tree," the *Sahdji* ballet, *Troubled Island,* and *Afro-American Symphony.*

The third period (1940–1978) was a combination of the first two, with some interesting twists. Here he composed his opera *Highway No. 1 U.S.A.* and his "Poem for Orchestra," which was commissioned by the Cleveland Orchestra.

Still was born in Woodville, Mississippi, on May 11, 1895. Both of his parents were musicians and his father was the town's bandmaster. Still received his early musical training at home. He attended the Oberlin College Conservatory of Music. In 1955, Still became the first African American to conduct a major orchestra in the Deep South when he led the New Orleans Symphony Orchestra. He was also the first Black to conduct a major American orchestra, performing his original work with the Los Angeles Philharmonic. He died in 1978.

With today's rising pride in African-American music, interest in Black classical composers like Still is skyrocketing. In the 1970s, Sister Elise, of the Catholic Order of the Sisters of the Blessed Sacrament, cofounded two Black opera companies: Opera/South and Opera Ebony. Opera/South featured Still's *Highway No. 1 U.S.A.* and "A Bayou Legend." In 1971, classical singer Natalie Hinderas recorded *Natalie Hinderas Plays Music by Black Composers* on Desto Records featuring Still's compositions. Dubbed the Dean of Black Classical Composers, Still's work remains as not only a reference point for some of the more contemporary African Americans in this genre, but also as a body of work that accurately reflected the times and Still's unique vision of the world.

Still had a number of firsts as an African-American composer; he wrote the first symphony and opera to be performed by a major American orchestra and opera company, respectively. He was also the first African American to conduct a major orchestra in the South.

HENRY OSSAWA TANNER

LIKE SO MANY TALENTED
AFRICAN-AMERICAN ARTISTS,
WORLD-CLASS PAINTER HENRY
OSSAWA TANNER HAD TO LEAVE
THE UNITED STATES TO GET
WIDESPREAD ACCEPTANCE. HIS
AWARD-WINNING SPIRITUAL ART IS
COMPARED TO RELIGIOUS
PAINTERS REMBRANDT
AND RUBENS.

A religious painter who swept the French off their feet at the turn of the century, Henry Ossawa Tanner was an African American who overcame incredible personal and racial obstacles to create beautiful art, which today is still proudly exhibited.

Tanner was born in Pittsburgh, Pennsylvania, in 1859. His father was an African Methodist Episcopal bishop. By his early teens, Tanner had already made up his mind that his life's work would be that of a great painter. His vocational inspiration came from an artist he once saw working in the field. But it seems that his spiritual inspiration came from his home, where his minister father played a pivotal role.

When his career finally started to get off the ground, he was bothered, like many other artists, with financial and health problems. He was forced to stop and restart his career several times.

Tanner decided his natural talent needed formal instruction if he were ever going to get past selling his paintings for $15 and watching them bring in $250 days later. He became a student at the Pennsylvania Academy for Fine Arts in Philadelphia, where from 1879 to 1885 he endured harassment from White students. Before the Academy for Fine Arts reluctantly accepted Tanner, other Philadelphia art teachers had rejected his work merely because he was Black.

Forced to take a job in the flour business, the overworked, underpaid artist seldom painted and was overwhelmed with health woes. In an attempt to jump-start his career, Tanner sent his artwork to New York publishers. He always received rejection letters, until one day a $40 check arrived. Soon he received an $80 check for his work; then came a job as an art instructor at Atlanta's Clark College.

With hope of succeeding in Europe, Tanner put on an exhibition to raise money. It was a failure. With a borrowed $75 in his pocket, Black themes in his work, dreams in his head, and paintbrushes under his arm, he boarded a boat to Italy. But he made a stop in Paris and didn't leave. It took him five years to finally get a painting sold to the Salon, for "Daniel in the Lions' Den." But in 1906, even his beloved Salon awarded Tanner only the second-class gold medal for "The Disciples at Emmanus," "since the first-class gold medal was reserved

only for French artists," said Tanner's biographers in a 1992 book published by the Philadelphia Museum of Art, *Henry Ossawa Tanner.*

Tanner's next expedition took the biblical painter to the Holy Land. He used the ancient backdrop for his artwork, including "Christ and Nicodemus" and "The Repentance of St. Peter."

France became his new home. And why not? He was insulted when he returned to America. When Tanner arrived in Chicago to exhibit his work, the Art Institute's prestigious Cliff Dweller's Club, which made him a member, would not let him in the dining room when White ladies were present.

Meanwhile, he won major awards, such as the Walter Lippencott Prize in 1900, the Gold medal at the Panama-Pacific Exhibition at San Francisco in 1915, and he was named chevalier of the Legion of Honor by the French government. He died in Paris on May 25, 1937.

Susan L. Taylor began her public career in the 1960s as an actress with the Negro Ensemble Company. The birth of her daughter in 1969 caused her to give up acting so she could spend more time with her child. Taylor went into business, first becoming a licensed beautician and then creating her own cosmetics line, Nequai Cosmetics (named after her daughter).

Her expertise in cosmetology and the success of her business, along with her stunning beauty, caught the eye a year later of the editors of *Essence,* a magazine marketed to African-American women. That year, she worked as a freelance writer for the magazine. A year later, she was the beauty editor. From 1971 to 1980, she supervised both the fashion and beauty departments.

Since 1980, Taylor has served as the magazine's editor-in-chief. During her stewardship, circulation has grown. One of her chief responsibilities has been writing the monthly editorial, "In the Spirit." In this column, she shares her intimate thoughts on values and morals she feels are important. She talks about spirituality, and in doing so touches readers in all walks of life. It is that positive message, along with her truly impressive track record, that has made her famous. *In the Spirit* also became the title of her first book.

Her newest book, *Lessons in Living,* is an exploration of intimate themes and issues. It's a celebration of her successes, failures, fears, and triumphs. But most of all, the book is a testament to her faith and commitment.

In the early part of the book, Taylor confesses: "For years, I'd been racing through each day, not living my life, not owning it. I was driven, trying to cover all the bases at home and work while wrestling inwardly with insecurity. For some time, I'd been going round and round in tighter and tighter circles, arriving again and again at the same wordless pain. The people, places and predicaments changed, but the emotional landscape was always the same—stress, doubt and fear."

Later on in the book, Taylor reveals how she found peace in her life and how other people—famous and obscure—have also come to terms with calamity and triumphed.

SUSAN L. TAYLOR WENT FROM BEING A SINGLE MOTHER WITH A SMALL COSMETICS COMPANY TO BECOMING AN AUTHOR, INSPIRATIONAL SPEAKER, AND EDITOR-IN-CHIEF OF ESSENCE MAGAZINE.

She has received many awards, including the Women in Communications Matrix Award and an honorary doctorate of Humane Letters from Lincoln University. Since 1986, Taylor has served as vice president of Essence Communications, Inc. She launched a nationally syndicated television magazine show, which received rave reviews during its short time on the air. She has also added a personal touch in managing her magazine's editorial content, insisting that Blacks worldwide get coverage.

Taylor's personal life and her career have intersected on one theme: nurturing the spirit for personal and community growth. A passage in the last chapter of her book, *Lessons in Living,* captures her inspirational message: "More love is our only hope for the future. It is all we need. Without more love, we will keep shifting from one thing to another in a restless search for satisfaction and peace. But contentment can only be found through self-nurturance balanced with service to others. That is when our joy is full."

Right: *Taylor makes a stunning entrance at the 1995 Essence Awards, an annual ceremony presented by the magazine honoring the best in Black artistic endeavors.* Essence *hosts an annual music festival, featuring many popular Black musicians.*

A SUPPORTER OF

THE WOMEN'S AND CIVIL RIGHTS MOVEMENTS, MARY CHURCH TERRELL FOUGHT TO ORGANIZE MINORITY WOMEN AGAINST THE DOUBLE HARDSHIP OF RACISM AND SEXISM. SHE WAS ACTIVE WELL INTO HER OLD AGE IN SUCCESSFULLY OVERTURNING JIM CROW LAWS.

Mary Church Terrell waged a lifelong struggle against injustice in any form. She remained active in the struggle for civil and women's rights for 70 years, although born into a life of relative privilege. Active in many associations, Terrell also led the fight to desegregate the nation's capital, Washington, D.C., in the 1950s.

Mary Church was born in 1863 in Memphis. Her parents were former slaves. Her father, Robert R. Church, had a successful saloon business, along with some real estate holdings. Her mother, Louisa, ran a successful beauty salon. The Churches were prosperous enough to send her north to Ohio for a proper education.

Terrell earned her bachelor's degree in 1884 and her master's degree in 1888 from Oberlin College. This made her one of the first Black women in America to earn a graduate degree. Afterward, she toured and studied languages in Europe for two years before returning to America. She then married future judge Robert H. Terrell in 1891.

Oberlin offered Terrell a job that would have made her the first Black registrar at a White college. She turned it down to marry. However, she did accept an appointment to the Board of Education in Washington, D.C., in 1895. She had begun teaching in that school system in 1887. Terrell became the first Black woman to hold this type of position. She resigned from the school board post in 1901, but was reappointed in 1906 and served on the board until 1911.

Active in the women's rights struggle, she zealously organized minority women in the fight against racism and sexism. In 1892, she headed a newly formed group called the Colored Women's League. That organization combined with other Black women's organizations in 1896 to form the National Association of Colored Women.

Terrell was elected the first president of the group, which established kindergartens and day-care centers for Black working mothers. The organization also pushed for economic opportunity and voting rights for Black women. That work led Terrell to join forces with Susan B. Anthony and Jane Addams in the suffrage movement. Women were finally legislated the right to vote in 1920.

Terrell was also important in the international women's movement; she represented American delegations at congresses in Berlin, Zurich, and London. Usually the lone African American at these gatherings, she impressed fellow delegates by giving her addresses in fluent German and French, as well as in her native English.

Terrell was poised, intellectually gifted, and articulate. These traits put her in great demand as a speaker, a vocation she successfully enjoyed for about 30 years. She spoke eloquently on any number of topics, from racial injustice to crime and culture. Writing these speeches led Terrell to writing articles on the same themes, which were published both in America and abroad. The culmination of her writing career came in 1940 with the publication of her autobiography, *A Colored Woman in a White World.*

In 1909, Terrell was one of two Black women at the founding meeting of the NAACP. She also attended the 1910 meeting, which formalized the organization, and for many years served as vice president of the Washington, D.C., branch. During the presidential campaigns of 1920 and 1932, the Republican Party appointed Terrell to organize minority women in the East. However, her three crowning accomplishments didn't come until 1949, when Terrell was 86 years old.

She chaired the National Committee to Free the Ingrams, a family of Georgia sharecroppers accused of the murder of a White man. The incident was obviously self-defense.

Terrell appealed to the United Nations and Georgia's governor. The Ingrams were eventually freed. That same year, after a three-year battle, Terrell gained membership into the Washington, D.C., chapter of the American Association of University Women. Her membership ended the group's policy of excluding Blacks.

Finally, in 1949, Terrell chaired the newly organized Coordinating Committee for the Enforcement of District of Columbia Anti-Discrimination Laws. The "Lost Laws of 1872–73" prohibited discrimination in restaurants, but owners often ignored the laws. The group fought through the press, in negotiation, by picketing and boycotting, and in court to have the laws enforced.

For almost a year, Terrell had her group boycott department stores whose restaurants refused to serve Blacks. At the age of 90, supported by a cane, Terrell herself headed the picket lines. Several stores finally yielded, and in 1953 the U.S. Supreme Court upheld the laws thus forcing other restaurants to comply. Terrell had won.

She died shortly thereafter on July 24, 1954. Many schools and women's organizations throughout the country have since been named in her honor.

Well-educated, wealthy, and prominent, Terrell was one of Black America's first female upper-class activists. She disdained the role of socialite, which was the slot generally imposed in her day on any women of means. Instead, she used her position and connections to fight for equal rights for women and African Americans.

WILLIAM MONROE TROTTER

WILLIAM MONROE TROTTER

WAS ONE OF THE FIRST MAJOR MILITANT BLACK LEADERS OF THE 20TH CENTURY. EDITOR OF THE GUARDIAN NEWSPAPER AND COFOUNDER OF THE NIAGARA MOVEMENT, TROTTER WAS A VIGOROUS FOE OF WHITE SUPREMACY AND CONSERVATIVE, ACCOMMODATIONIST AFRICAN-AMERICAN LEADERS SUCH AS BOOKER T. WASHINGTON.

While turn-of-the-century Whites elevated Booker T. Washington as the "good Negro," *The Guardian* newspaper editor William Monroe Trotter was the militant Black leader at the time. He blossomed from a burgeoning newspaperman to become a significant thorn in the side of segregation and the champion of his people.

After President Woodrow Wilson said segregating government employees in federal bureaus was "in Blacks' best interest," Trotter, on November 12, 1914, marched into the White House. Trotter felt that for the president to say this at a time when there were many lynchings and other increased attacks against Blacks was not only calculating but downright "insulting." Virginia-born Wilson reportedly dismissed Trotter for shaking his finger at him.

Trotter had an interesting history for an African American at that time. He was born April 7, 1872, in Chillicothe, Ohio, but was raised in a predominantly White suburb. There he was steeled in the traditions of abolitionists.

Trotter's father, James, the Mississippi-born son of a White slave owner, was a federal officeholder under President Grover Cleveland. Trotter's father was successful in real estate. Trotter's mother was a fair-skinned woman related to Thomas Jefferson.

Raised in an upper-class Negro household, young Trotter was constantly admonished to do better than Whites as a means of breaking down color barriers. The lessons he learned from his parents helped him develop into a human rights activist filled with Black pride.

He started his work early. Trotter was the only African-American student in his high school class. He led the class academically and was elected student body president. His studiousness won him scholarships to Harvard College, which he entered in 1891. He was elected Phi Beta Kappa in his junior year— the first African American to earn that distinction at Harvard.

Trotter entered the real estate business after graduation. Racial problems he encountered pursuing that career led to his growing militancy. The Jim Crow segregation laws that swept the country at the turn of the century forced Trotter to move his business several times. He also had to make other frustrating, race-based concessions.

In 1901, to rail against such injustices, he started *The Guardian* newspaper in Boston with Amherst-trained George Forbes. Their newspaper was in the same building that housed William Lloyd Garrison's *Liberator,* an abolitionist newspaper that had the same message of total equality and total struggle.

Trotter launched his activist journal in part to show a viable alternative in Black leadership to the accommodationist Booker T. Washington. Trotter felt that Washington, the most high-profile Black leader of the day, was a traitor to the African-American cause. He believed that Washington consistently tried to paint American race relations and opportunities for Blacks in a better light than reality indicated.

Trotter constantly bashed Washington in *The Guardian*, portraying him as a self-serving political hypocrite. Trotter was able to agitate considerable public criticism against Washington in the Black community. Washington, in turn, filed several lawsuits against Trotter, while funding another newspaper that he hoped would be a rival to *The Guardian.*

This personal feud escalated and culminated in July 1903, when Trotter organized a disturbance, including hecklers, at a speech given by Washington in Boston. The disturbance turned into a riot. Trotter was arrested and served a 30-day jail term.

Washington's intimidation seemed to work in reverse, though, firing up this incendiary activist even more. He helped make Trotter a hero in the Black community among those favoring Trotter's more militant views over the accommodating leanings of Washington.

Trotter teamed up with W.E.B. Du Bois, another Harvard-educated Black, and African-American feminist social worker Ida B. Wells. Together, they formed the Niagara Movement in 1905 in Niagara Falls, Ontario. It became the forerunner of the NAACP. Trotter and Du Bois's work also reinvigorated the Black press and was a key influence in reviving the protest movement among African Americans.

Trotter, with his editorials in *The Guardian,* and Du Bois, with his columns in *The Crisis,* were two men of letters who created a new, intellectual-based journalism.

Trotter attended the founding conference of the NAACP in 1909. But, while Du Bois became an instrumental force in the organization, Trotter never embraced it because he could not go along with the White money and White leadership that directed the NAACP.

Instead, he founded the National Equal Rights League. However, as the NAACP grew, Trotter's leadership declined.

He died on his 62nd birthday in 1934. He left his mark as one of the 20th century's first militant Black leaders.

Trotter was a tenacious, militant bulldog of a journalist who dared to question the conservative Black leadership of the day through his newspaper, The Guardian. *He even shook his finger in the face of the president of the United States for segregating Black federal employees.*

SOJOURNER TRUTH

Sojourner Truth was an ex-slave who used her experience and her faith to convince others of slavery's cruelties. She will best be remembered as an abolitionist, suffragist, and feminist. For more than 40 years, Sojourner Truth was also a preacher and a teacher. The great and the near-great sang her praises and quoted her strong and striking utterances.

Truth believed it was her Christian duty to further the cause of Black people. That sense of duty won her an audience with President Abraham Lincoln. Ushered into Lincoln's presence October 29, 1864, she showered him with unabashed praise. Truth assured him in a deep-toned voice that he was the greatest president this country ever had, a man to be likened unto Daniel, the biblical standard of courage and faithfulness.

Sojourner Truth and Harriet Tubman were twin mountain peaks of the tradition of Black women. These deeply religious women practiced what they preached. They honored the human rights of Black people, many of whom were held in the bonds of slavery.

Born Isabella Bomefree in Ulster County, New York, in 1797, Sojourner Truth had a succession of cruel slave masters. One took her away from her parents; another sold her youngest child away from her. He illegally transported her son to Alabama.

Truth showed her resiliency and strength of character by attaining the assistance of Quakers in Ulster County, who helped her successfully sue to have her son returned. This was one of Truth's first and most dramatic efforts to show that she would not be broken by the tyranny of slavery. The next year, 1827, Truth herself became free under New York's Gradual Emancipation Act.

Experiencing a religious conversion the same year, she joined the African Zion Church and became an inspired preacher at camp meetings around the New York area. In 1843, tiring of urban life and feeling the need to spread her message to a larger audience, she walked out of New York City. All she had was a bag of clothes, 25 cents, and a new name: Sojourner Truth.

"The Lord," she said, "gave me the name Sojourner because I was to travel up and down this land showing people their sins and being a sign to them. Afterwards I told the Lord I wanted another name 'cause everybody else had two names; and the Lord gave me Truth, because I was to declare truth onto people." That is exactly what she did for four decades. On a platform, Truth was amazing.

Though illiterate, she had the persuasive power that reduced seemingly complicated matters to their essentials.

On one occasion, a proslavery heckler told her, "Old woman, why I don't care any more for your antislavery talk than I do a bite from a flea." Truth smiled and candidly replied, "Perhaps not, but the good Lord willing, I'll keep you scratching."

She refused to let antagonists stop her. In doing so, Truth helped define womanhood in a way that embraced the African-American women's experience. "Nobody ever helps me into carriages, or over mudpuddles, or gives me any best place!" she declared at a women's rights convention in Akron, Ohio, in 1851. "Ain't I a woman?"

Another famous incident in which she proved her womanhood occurred in 1858. She stood up to a heckler who asked whether she was a man or woman; he believed she was far too smart to be female. Truth opened her blouse and referred to her work as a slave wet nurse.

Wearing her trademark turban and sunbonnet, Truth walked the land for more than 40 years. She supported herself through lecture fees, the sale of personal items, and the sale of the book *The Narrative of Sojourner Truth*. The book was written by abolitionist Olive Gilbert, and Truth published it herself.

Sojourner Truth proudly broke the taboos about women speaking in public by preaching, teaching, and testifying about the rights of both African Americans and women. Truth had a stunning presence and a searing message. She died November 26, 1883, in Battle Creek, Michigan.

For 40 years, from 1843 to her death in 1883, Sojourner Truth walked the land spreading her message of opposition to slavery and support of women's rights. She is an African-American legend.

HARRIET TUBMAN

Probably the best known conductor on the Underground Railroad, Harriet Tubman's life was dedicated to freedom. With stops in the South, the Underground Railroad operated primarily in New England and the Ohio Western Reserve, where secrecy in helping runaway slaves was essential in the pre–Civil War era.

Tubman also was the first and possibly the last woman to lead U.S. Army troops into battle. Working in South Carolina and other states, Tubman organized slave intelligence networks behind enemy lines and led scouting raids.

A graphic account of the battle she led appeared in the *Boston Commonwealth* July 10, 1863. In glowing language, the article noted how Colonel Montgomery and his gallant band of 150 Black soldiers, under Tubman's guidance, dashed into the enemy's country. They destroyed millions of dollars' worth of commissary stores, cotton, and lordly dwellings, "and struck terror into the heart of rebeldom, brought off near 800 slaves and thousands of dollars worth of property, without losing a man or receiving a scratch."

Despite working for four years off and on in the service of the Union Army as a nurse, spy, and scout, Tubman was never duly rewarded after the war. Yet she was never bitter. She was a true humanitarian. A big-souled, God-intoxicated, heroic Black woman, Tubman's mission was saving others. She spent the last two decades of her life, however, in virtual poverty. She was a woman with a mission and that mission guided her to freedom, and back into slave states where she brilliantly planned and executed escapes for hundreds of slaves.

At great personal risk, Tubman led many to freedom with an operation that she funded primarily by her work as a domestic. In doing so, Tubman inspired peers and future generations of African-American women to continue the long-standing tradition of self-help and self-improvement prevalent in the Black community.

Dark-complexioned and short, Tubman had a full, broad face and she often wore a colorful head bonnet. She developed almost extraordinary physical endurance and muscular strength as well as mental fortitude. She was unpretentious, practical, shrewd, and visionary. A deeply religious woman with a driven sense of purpose, she credited the Almighty and not herself for guiding her during dangerous journeys. She also had a superstitious side, believing deeply in dreams and omens that seemed to put a protective umbrella over her perilous exploits.

She was born on a slave-breeding plantation in Maryland about 1821, one of 11 children of Harriet and Benjamin Ross. Originally named Araminta, she was renamed Harriet by her mother. In an attempt to stop a nearby runaway slave, Tubman's master threw a two-pound weight on her head as a child. The weight crushed her skull and caused her sleeping fits and headaches that later plagued her all her life. After the master died, it was rumored that the slaves were to be sent to the Deep South.

Fearing the often deadly consequences of such a move south, Tubman and two of her brothers decided to escape. Fearful of what would happen if they were apprehended, her brothers turned back but Harriet kept walking to freedom. She later returned to get three of her brothers and returned again to get her mother and father. Infuriated slave masters offered a $40,000 reward for her capture, dead or alive.

Said Tubman: "There was one or two things I had right to, liberty or death; if I could not have one, I would have the other; for no man should take me alive; I should fight for my liberty as long as my strength lasted, and when the time come for to go, the Lord would let them take me."

For her heroic work, Tubman received many honors, including a medal from Queen Victoria of England. When she received a $20 monthly pension for her nursing services during the Civil War, she used the money to help needy, elderly freed men and women.

Tubman died in Auburn, New York, on March 10, 1913. After her death, a campaign was launched to collect funds for a monument in the town square. The monument stands in testimony to her of indomitable will.

Shrewd and tough both mentally and physically, Tubman is possibly the only woman to have led U.S. Army troops in battle, which she did in the Civil War with Union soldiers. In addition to her heroic work on the Underground Railroad, where she conducted slaves to freedom, Tubman also served the Union Army as a nurse, scout, and spy. Tubman (seated, right) is pictured below with her family.

HENRY McNEAL TURNER

The Black church has always been and probably always will be the most autonomous institution within the African-American community. Never was the influence of the Black church so powerful as during the late days of slavery.

It is said that of all the groups and individuals working with the missionary movement to aid southern Blacks, none were more important than the northern churches of free Blacks. Not only did they collect money, clothes, and food, but they also sent social workers and teachers to their downtrodden brothers and sisters languishing under the harsh dictate of southern slavery.

One of the most famous leaders of the Black clergy was the Rev. Henry McNeal Turner of Israel Church in Washington, D.C. He was born in Abbeville, South Carolina, in 1834. Like most militant Black intellectuals at the time, Turner was educated in the North. He studied to be a minister. Turner used his pulpit to urge his parishioners to join the Union Army. In 1863, shortly after Turner's historic report about the jubilant effect of President Lincoln's Emancipation Proclamation on Blacks and Whites, Lincoln made him chaplain of the Black troops. President Andrew Johnson made him a chaplain in the Regular Army in 1865.

Following the end of the Civil War, Turner went to Georgia, working in the African Methodist Episcopal Church—a church founded by Blacks who were denied worship by Whites. After the passage of the Reconstruction Acts, he became a member of the Georgia State Legislature, but only after a bitter fight, which lasted from 1868 to 1870. The fight left him battered publicly, but he was still defiant. He was finally seated in the statehouse as a Republican despite attempts by White Democrats to prevent it. In defense of himself and 23 other Black representatives who were temporarily being denied their rightful seat in the Georgia legislature, Turner made a historic speech before the body that began at 9 A.M. and ended six hours later. He said, "We are told that if Black men want to speak, they must speak through White trumpets!" Turner and the others were finally admitted in 1869.

But by 1876, radical Reconstruction in the South was dead.

In the next few decades, disenchanted with the increasing White supremacy, Turner and others found refuge in theories bandied about by Pan-Africanists who felt life for Blacks in America was futile. He and other emigrationists, including Edward Wilmot Blydon, called their concept "Africa for the Africans." Turner called for "two or three million" Blacks to return "to the land of our ancestors, and establish our own nation, civilization, laws, customs, style of manufacture, and not only give the world, like other race varieties, the benefit of our individuality, but build up social conditions peculiarly our own." Despite his passionate leadership in the back-to-Africa concept, Turner preferred the word "Negro" to "African" when speaking about Blacks in the Western Hemisphere.

Refusing to die on American soil, Turner died in 1915, in Windsor, Ontario, Canada.

Facing page: *After the Civil War, Turner was assigned as an agent of the Freedmen's Bureau in Georgia, but quit to organize area churches as a base from which to help freed slaves participate in politics. He also served as president of Morris Brown College in Atlanta for 12 years. Above: Turner (seated center in first row) on April 18, 1898, with delegates to the Transvaal Annual Conference, which he organized.*

NAT TURNER

NAT TURNER

WAS EITHER A HERO OR A MADMAN. IN 1831, TURNER LED A VIOLENT INSURRECTION AGAINST WHITES IN SOUTHAMPTON COUNTY, VIRGINIA. THE REPERCUSSIONS LED TO THE MAJOR DEBATES OVER SLAVERY THAT EVENTUALLY IGNITED THE CIVIL WAR.

Nat Turner said he felt the pain and horror of slaves like him who were kidnapped, raped, abused, and tortured. So he set out with his band of insurgents and killed 60 Whites. That insurrection stirred slave owners to increase atrocities on slaves to teach any would-be Nat Turners a lesson.

To some, he avenged the Holocaust bestowed on his fellow Blacks by Whites who were profiting from human flesh. To others, Turner was a demented madman who left a trail of terror in which he and his followers killed about 60 Whites in a rebellion in Southampton County, Virginia, in 1831.

Ironically, Turner, who was born a slave in Southampton County in 1800, managed to escape when he was 21. But he returned to his master, he said, because of religious convictions.

Like most men with a mission, Nat Turner came to the view early in his life that God chose him for a purpose. He believed that purpose was to lead an uprising against slavery. To prepare himself for his mission, he kept to himself, fasted, prayed, and avoided crowds, tobacco, liquor, and money. By the time he reached maturity, he was well respected among slaves.

He was known to pray by the plow, and some say he saw visions and heard voices. One vision showed Black and White spirits fighting in the sky until the sun darkened and streams ran with blood. What happened that day was a solar eclipse, but Turner believed it was his sign to begin the uprising.

Turner chose his disciples and, after much preparation and prayer, he met them in a wooded retreat near his cruel slave master's farm. Under the cloak of darkness on the morning of August 22, they attacked the slave master, named Joseph Travis, hacking him and his family of five to death.

For the next 40 hours, the group, originally consisting of seven slave rebels, rampaged. They went from house to house, village to village, gathering more slave warriors on the way as they liberated several zones in Southampton County. They sent slave owners and traders to hell, while gleefully singing the praises of bloody insurrection. No Whites were spared except poor families who owned no slaves.

News spread quickly over the state of Virginia and surrounding areas. Soon, some 3,000 armed Whites, including soldiers from as far away as North Carolina, converged in Southampton. The troops committed atrocities, slaying innocent Blacks at will—as many as 200 in Southampton alone. That was apparently the point—not to put down the insurrection but to terrorize the slave population so they would never rise again against their White masters.

In fact, on September 3, 1831, the Richmond *Constitutional Whig* verified that fact. An editorial said that if another such insurrection should happen, it will be a "signal for the extermination of the whole Black population." Slave revolts could be directly linked to laws that legalized branding, burning, hamstringing, amputation, and death to slaves who resisted captivity.

Turner was finally caught on October 30 of that year. On November 11, this bold Black man, who some called Prophet, dangled from a tree as if he were a strange fruit.

Turner's death was a turning point in America. The major slavery debates raged from that point on until the abolition of this inhuman practice was ended by a bitter war that tore the nation in two. The same year that Turner's insurgents spread Black hope and White fear, William Lloyd Garrison established his inflammatory *Liberator* newspaper. Abolitionists also organized the New England Antislavery Society that year.

Twenty years later, a White man with a mission named John Brown would set out on the same path. He bellowed Nat Turner's name as he traveled freedom's road only to find his liberty, like Turner's, at the end of a rope.

This illustration depicts the capture of Nat Turner, who hid out for five weeks after leading a slave revolt in Southampton, Virginia, in 1831. Turner was hanged for his part in the rebellion.

The incredible story of African-American aviators in World War II began on a lone Alabama runway at Tuskegee Army Air Field on March 21, 1941, with the activation and construction of a segregated airfield for the 99th Pursuit Squadron.

On March 7, 1942, five pilots stood on the runway at graduation exercises, poised to take their place in aviation history. First Lady

Eleanor Roosevelt took a flight with Black pilot Dr. Charles Alfred Anderson to show her official support for the program that detractors said would never get off the ground.

This airfield came at a time when African Americans were shackled by legal White su-

premacy in the South and racial exclusion in the North, and any act of so-called disrespect could result in injury or death. Learning how to fly, to many Whites and a few Blacks, was one such act of disrespect.

African Americans up to that time had routinely and rudely been excluded from the Army Air Force because there were no established Black units. There were persistent myths that Blacks were incompetent to fly and also lacked the intellectual skills to do so. Yet, there were more than 100 Black pilots at the time. Two bold Black pilots 20 years prior, Eugene Bullard and Bessie Coleman, had learned to fly in France. They inspired a whole new generation of African-American aviators. At least two Black schools developed: the Bessie Coleman Aero Club in Los Angeles and the Coffey School of Aeronautics at the Harlem Airport in Oak Lawn, near Chicago.

Under the leadership of Lieutenant Colonel Benjamin Davis, Jr., the Tuskegee Airmen

THE TUSKEGEE AIRMEN WERE BRAVE BLACK FIGHTER PILOTS WHO HAD TO FIGHT DISCRIMINATION AT HOME AS WELL AS NAZI AGGRESSION ABROAD. THEY HELPED WIN ON BOTH FRONTS.

had their first taste of combat against the highly fortified island of Pentelleria. The successful attack of the island proved that Blacks could be triumphant in battle.

Subsequent successful battles in Europe and Africa proved the Tuskegee Airmen's talents and abilities. They also substantiated the Black aviators' contention that given the opportunity, Black fighter pilots could be every bit as good if not better than their White counterparts. Captain Luke Weathers scored two victories in one day. Another of the many heroes was Lieutenant Clarence D. Lester, whose bomber formation was attacked by 30 or more ME–109 and FW–190 enemy planes on July 18, 1944. Piloting a P–51 aircraft en route to enemy installations in Germany, Lester engaged with the enemy planes. He destroyed three enemy fighters "thus materially aiding in preventing the enemy from making concentrated attacks on American bombers," Lester's citation read, when he was decorated for outstanding bravery in battle.

On July 26, 1948, President Truman issued two executive orders desegregating the military, thanks in part to the heroic efforts of the brave Black Tuskegee Airmen.

Facing page: *The success of the Tuskegee Airmen in engaging the Nazi Air Force during World War II helped lead to the desegregation of the American military, by executive order of President Harry Truman in 1948.*
Above: *Lieutenant Colonel Benjamin Davis, Jr. (standing on wing), son of Brigadier General Benjamin Davis and leader of the Tuskegee Airmen, gives final instructions to Lieutenant Charles W. Dryden in 1943.*

ALICE WALKER

Writer Alice Walker paved the way for both Black and women authors when her Pulitzer Prize-winning novel *The Color Purple* was developed into a Steven Spielberg film. It received 11 Academy Award nominations. Her books have sold millions of copies and have been translated into two dozen languages.

While the controversial and popular book *The Color Purple*, which examines the effects of domestic violence and racism on three generations of southern Black farmers, is her most famous work, it is one of many important pieces penned by this self-described "womanist" writer. Other noteworthy works include *The Temple of My Familiar, The Third Life of Grange Copeland,* and *Possessing the Secret of Joy.* Her newest work, *Crossing the Same River Twice,* has received favorable reviews and lots of attention—something Walker enjoys professionally yet shuns in her personal life.

This reflective feminist writer was the youngest of eight children. She was born in 1944, in Eatonton, Georgia. Her father was a sharecropper and her mother was a maid.

Walker said both her parents were strong storytellers, and she remembers her mother toiling to make their humble shack spotless.

Like other important writers, Walker's childhood had pivotal events that changed her forever. At age eight, she got shot in the eye with a BB bullet by one of her brothers. Because her family did not own a car, Walker was forced to wait a week before a doctor examined her. The doctor then told her she was permanently blind. Self-conscious and shy, Walker, who had been an outgoing youth, retreated to a private world of words, ideas, and books. She started writing poetry and became so proficient she was awarded several fellowships. She was also offered the opportunity to have her poems published.

Some critics speculate that Walker's own mutilation helped her identify with Tashi, the main character in *Possessing the Secret of Joy.* Tashi is a tribal African woman who was genitally mutilated by the tsunga's knife and severely traumatized because of the experience. She spends the rest of her life fighting madness and is treated by disciples of both

Freud and Jung, and even Jung himself. Finally, she regains her ability to feel. This book has generated much controversy—critics of Walker say African cultural rituals are not America's concern. Feminists and many others say mutilation of women is not about culture but about control of women.

After high school, Walker attended Spelman College in Atlanta and Sarah Lawrence College in Bronxville, New York, where she graduated. Her first job after college was working in the Welfare Department in New York City. She hated the job and wrote feverishly at night. After leaving the Welfare Department, she was writer in residence and professor of Black studies at Jackson State College and Tougaloo College in Mississippi. Her night writing paid off in 1970 when she published her first novel, *The Third Life of Grange Copeland*, about sharecroppers. She would soon revisit the same theme with *The Color Purple*. Walker continues to write.

Left: *As a child, Walker wanted something far different than the sharecropping world she knew. She dreamed of being a painter or blues singer.* Right: *Walker ended up in the world of words and ideas. Her work with and mastery of words has earned her many awards, including a Pulitzer Prize.*

MADAM C. J. WALKER

MADAM C. J. WALKER

REVOLUTIONIZED THE HAIR-CARE INDUSTRY FOR BLACKS IN THE EARLY 1900S WHEN SHE INVENTED A HAIR STRAIGHTENING PROCESS. SHE EMPLOYED MORE THAN 3,000 SALES AGENTS AND AMASSED A FORTUNE THAT MADE HER AMERICA'S FIRST BLACK MILLIONAIRE.

After 38 years of a humble life where she and her daughter lived virtually hand-to-mouth, Madam C. J. Walker perfected a hair-care formula. It was so popular with African Americans of the early 20th century that she became this country's first Black female millionaire and a pioneer in the cosmetics industry. Though she became one of the most famous African Americans of her time, sadly, she enjoyed her business success for only 14 years before her death.

She was born Sarah Breedlove in Delta, Louisiana, on December 23, 1867. Her parents were poor farmers and former slaves. She lived in a run-down shack on a plantation on the Mississippi River. The house had no toilet or running water, and the family slept on the dirt floor. Walker picked cotton from sunup to sunset until she was orphaned at age seven. She then went to Mississippi, where she lived with an older sister.

At the age of 14, Walker married to escape the cruelties of her sister's husband. Her own husband was killed when she was 20, leaving her alone to raise her two-year-old daughter, A'Lelia. For the next 18 years, Walker worked as a washerwoman in St. Louis to support them. Although she could not read or write at the time, she saved her small earnings and sent A'Lelia to Knoxville College. Despite her future success, this single act remained one of her proudest accomplishments.

Walker found herself going bald and she began experimenting with medicines and secret ingredients to try to nurse her hair back to health. In 1905, she developed a formula, with sulphur as a main ingredient, that not only stopped her hair loss but also enabled her hair to grow back quickly. It also could straighten curly Black hair when used with a hot comb.

Walker always said that the formula came to her in a dream after she prayed to God to save her hair. Some ingredients in the recipe that appeared to her in the dream were grown in Africa, so Walker sent for them. She prepared the concoction and after applying it, she found her hair growing back in faster than it had fallen out. Walker then began selling this pomade preparation, which she called a "miracle hair grower," to friends and neighbors.

After her brother died, she moved to Denver to stay with her sister-in-law. She continued to sell her product to local Black women. Then, she decided to put the $1.50 she had to her name into buying the necessary chemicals and manufacturing her pomade in jars. Walker was now a businesswoman, not a laborer.

She soon met newspaperman Charles Walker, whom she married. He brought his expertise in advertising to the operation. Now Madam C. J. Walker, she put ads in Black publications. She also began a profitable mail-order arm of her business.

Personally showing her styling methods door-to-door throughout the South and East, she opened beauty schools and trained agents. These agents started their own businesses selling her products. Walker also developed a steel comb for Black hair that could be heated on a stove.

The success of her hair-care treatment system rested in the versatility of styling that it offered African-American women who wanted different hairstyles. The Walker System became an international success when Josephine Baker (who sang mostly in France) used it. This success prompted the French to develop their own pomade.

Walker and her daughter became wealthy and opened cosmetic colleges in Pittsburgh and New York and a plant in Indianapolis. They built and lived in a mansion in New York called Villa Lewaro.

The Walkers gave more than 3,000 Black women the opportunity to leave domestic work and become entrepreneurs. These sales agents learned how to set up beauty parlors in their homes, keep business records, and become financially independent.

Though Walker and her daughter became prominent socialites and patrons of the arts, they used much of their money to benefit others. Madam Walker contributed freely to the NAACP and funded scholarships for young women at Tuskegee Institute.

Madam Walker died May 25, 1919, at Villa Lewaro.

Walker was not only America's first Black female millionaire, it's also believed that she was the first woman in the country to reach that economic level through entrepreneurship instead of by inheritance. She made her fortune by inventing a revolutionary hair straightening formula for African-American women with naturally curly hair.

Booker T. Washington

WILL ALWAYS BE FONDLY REMEMBERED AS FOUNDER OF TUSKEGEE INSTITUTE, A BLACK COLLEGE IN ALABAMA THAT LAUNCHED THE CAREERS OF THOUSANDS OF BLACKS. WASHINGTON WAS AN EX-SLAVE WHO MAY HAVE BEEN THE MOST POWERFUL BLACK MAN IN U.S. HISTORY.

At the turn of the century, Booker Taliaferro Washington was simultaneously the most powerful and the most controversial Black leader of his time.

His supporters say he tirelessly toiled for Black pride and educational and economic advancement and that he used his influence with White industrialists to get huge amounts of money for Black colleges. His critics say he cozied up to the White power structure, using federal patronage and the favor of White philanthropists to create his own political machine. Historians say they are both right.

Washington was born a mulatto slave in 1856 on a small Virginia farm. He spent his early years of freedom working in coal mines and salt furnaces. He attended Freedmen's Bureau School and Hampton Institute, then a secondary and industrial school.

In 1881, Washington founded Tuskegee Institute in the Black belt of Alabama—something many cite as his crowning achievement because of the thousands of Blacks whose careers were made possible thanks to the opportunity they were afforded at Tuskegee. The school specialized in vocational and agricultural careers—jobs nonthreatening to an increasingly hostile White workforce.

Washington spent the next 15 years building this landmark institution by accommodating local Whites and raising money from northern ones, who were attracted to his emphasis on thrift, hard work, and good moral character. They viewed industrial education as no threat to southern White labor.

At this time, militant abolitionist Frederick Douglass was deemed the most articulate Black spokesman. Douglass died in 1895, the same year that Washington catapulted into national fame with a speech known as the Atlanta Compromise Address delivered at the Cotton States and International Exposition. In

Washington's speech, he implied a scaling back in Black voting rights in favor of White support for Black business. He used the parable of the open hand and the empty bucket to illustrate his point.

His accommodationist, self-help philosophy was clarified in his *Up From Slavery* autobiography published in 1901. The book quickly became a best-seller and Washington a household word. He was constantly hailed as a "credit to his race." It even earned him a White House audience with President Theodore Roosevelt that same year, and he remained an important advisor to the president. Washington then perfected his political prowess by building an organization that more often than not yielded principle to expediency. Washington secretly funded lawyers and pressed court suits to protest segregation in public transportation and prevent Black sharecroppers from being driven from their land. He maneuvered bad situations and made them work for him. Perhaps that was his greatest skill.

His program of industrial education and promotion of small business as the primary way Blacks could move up the ladder might have seemed pragmatic, given the racial hatred that existed at that time. But critics

then and today cite it as taking people of African descent several steps backward. One critic of the Atlanta Compromise speech was noted educator John Hope. "I regard it as cowardly and dishonest for any of our colored men to tell White people or colored people that we are not struggling for equality."

Others praised Washington's industrial philosophy. Industrialist Andrew Carnegie and feminist Susan B. Anthony were among the most prominent speakers who appeared at Tuskegee Institute. Washington's biographer Louis R. Harlan said that Washington "worked

Facing page: Washington was a powerful, controversial Black leader who admonished African Americans to pull themselves up by their own bootstraps in order to overcome the limitations placed on them by a racist society. The accommodationist leader outwardly preached a philosophy of going along to get along. But often, in secret, he funded lawsuits to protest segregation and to help Black sharecroppers keep their land. Above: *Washington speaks at an Armstrong Association meeting held at a packed Carnegie Hall.*

unceasingly" for Black pride, material advancement, and every kind of education. "He did these things more by private action than ringing declaration."

Washington's most vocal critic at the time was W.E.B. Du Bois, the Harvard-educated philosopher-activist-writer who called for "ceaseless agitation" as opposed to Washington's "go along, get along" line. According to Du Bois, "It wasn't a matter of ideals or anything of that sort. With everything that Washington met, he evidently had the idea: 'Now, What's your racket?'" Washington's rule was "bossism." He rewarded his friends and punished his enemies. He used spies, bribes, and anything else short of violence to bring down opponents, who mainly came from the progressive quarters of the Black community. Meanwhile, poverty, lynchings, and other assaults to the human dignity of Blacks flourished at the hands of southern and northern Whites who in the 1890s began a movement to take back all the rights Blacks had achieved.

A little known fact about Washington is that in his final years he addressed many of the civil rights questions that the NAACP had raised and he had previously rejected. In his last few years, Washington differed from their approach, not their goal.

Washington's supporter, William H. Lewis, memorialized his mentor by saying: "He knew the Southern White man better than the Southern White man knew himself, and knew the sure road to his head and heart."

At age 59, Washington died in 1915 after a long illness at Tuskegee. Three days after his death, one of the largest crowds in the Institute's history gathered to honor him.

Washington's successor was Robert R. Moten, his former secretary. Moten was more accommodating to the protest movement, signaling that it may now be acceptable for some of Washington's old supporters to join forces with the NAACP. Ironically, in the Depression era of the 1930s, W.E.B. Du Bois, Washington's old antagonist, advocated economic policies similar to those proposed by Washington. This caused a spilt between Du Bois and Walter F. White within the ranks of the NAACP.

Washington will forever remain a controversial figure. Each small community and hamlet would create their own Washington, a Black man who could speak to his community and for his community as the voice of Negro opinion. On the other hand, Washington remains admired by many Black nationalists and Black radicals, who view him as a symbol of Black empowerment, "doing for self."

IDA B. WELLS-BARNETT

A JOURNALIST AND CIVIL RIGHTS LEADER, IDA B. WELLS-BARNETT FEARLESSLY FOUGHT FOR BLACK SELF-RELIANCE AND AGAINST THE VIOLENCE AND ECONOMIC REPRESSION THAT HAVE KEPT AFRICAN AMERICANS AND WOMEN IN OPPRESSION.

Ida B. Wells-Barnett was a formidable force in the battle for equality and economic parity for Blacks. She was nicknamed a "crusader for justice" by the people. Wells-Barnett's scathing editorials against lynching and White violence against Blacks alerted the country to the atrocities common in the post-Reconstruction South. Wells-Barnett spent her life lecturing against discrimination and injustice, and she exhorted Blacks to use their economic power to change racist White behavior.

Wells-Barnett was born a slave in Mississippi, in 1862, to a family with a strong faith in education. Her parents died of yellow fever in 1878, and the young teenager began teaching so she could care for her siblings. Later, Wells-Barnett moved to Memphis, Tennessee, which turned out to be the beginning of a lifelong quest for equality.

In 1884, Wells-Barnett refused to accept a seat in a Jim Crow car, then filed an unsuccessful lawsuit against the railroad company. Her militant actions, along with some editorials critical of inadequate African-American schools, caused her to lose her teaching job.

Wells-Barnett then launched a career of using her mighty pen to call the country to task for its treatment of Blacks.

After editing several small Black papers, Wells-Barnett became part-owner of the Memphis *Free Speech and Headlight.* In 1892, three Black men were lynched because their business was competing with a White firm. Wells-Barnett fired off a series of blistering editorials, accusing Whites of using lynching to punish financially indepedent African Americans. She declared that "neither character nor standing avails the Negro if he dares to protect himself from the White man or become his rival." Furious Whites burned down her paper's presses and threatened her life if she returned to the South.

Undaunted, Wells-Barnett moved to New York, continuing her angry attacks on lynching at militant journalist T. Thomas Fortune's *New York Age.* She published pamphlets on the lynching problem and traveled overseas, drumming up international outrage.

This tireless crusader helped form and worked with many important groups, including the National Association of Colored Women, The Ida B. Wells Club, and the Negro Fellowship League. Wells-Barnett was also instrumental in creating the National Association for the Advancement of Colored People.

Wells-Barnett moved to Chicago in 1893, where she published a pamphlet denouncing the exclusion of Blacks from the World's Fair. She married lawyer and Chicago Conservator founder Ferdinand Barnett in 1895, and together they were formidable champions for Black civil rights. Wells-Barnett continued her fight against lynching, also taking on the issues of segregated schools in Chicago and the importance of Black female community involvement.

Wells-Barnett's voice was finally silenced on March 25, 1931, when she died in Chicago of uremic poisoning. She remains a jewel in the crown of the struggle for equality.

Left: *Wells-Barnett was a crusading journalist who become one of the nation's foremost authorities on the atrocity of lynching.* Right: *Her lifespan, from 1862 to 1931, coincided with the stretch of time in America when lynchings were at their zenith. Through her many studies and documentations, Wells-Barnett estimated the number of Blacks killed by lynching to be in the tens of thousands.*

PHILLIS WHEATLEY

A young slave stolen from her native Senegal village in Africa at the age of seven or eight, Phillis Wheatley is the mother of the African-American literary tradition. She was the first Black to publish a book—a collection of poems—and only the second woman in the United States to publish a book of poetry. In the process, she became almost an icon to abolitionists trying to prove that Blacks and Whites were intellectual equals if given equal opportunities.

Twas mercy brought me from my Pagan
    land,
Taught my benighted soul to understand
That there's a God, that there's a Savior
    too:
Once I redemption neither fought nor
    knew.
Some view our fable race with scornful
    eye,
"their colour is a diabolic die."
Remember Christians, Negros black as
    Cain,
May be refin'd and join th' angelic train.

Wheatley's poem "On Being Brought from Africa to America" was part of a series of works published in her 1773 book, *Poems on Various Subjects, Religious and Moral.* Except for a single poem published in 1760 by Jupiter Hammon, another slave, Wheatley's book was the first published by an African American. She most often wrote her poems, mostly elegies and honorific verse, to commemorate the life and death of friends, famous contemporaries, and important events. She wrote her poetry in a style and with references that reflected her African heritage.

Wheatley's writings set off a storm of criticism, both by those who couldn't believe that a Black woman was capable of creative thought and by those who saw her as a Black genius and proof that African Americans were not intellectually inferior to Whites. Before *Poems on Various Subjects* was first published, the fact that Wheatley had written it was considered so extraordinary that 18 of Boston's movers and shakers questioned her to prove that she had written the poems. When *Poems* was published in 1773, it began with a signed "Attestation" by these men, including John Hancock and the Massachusetts governor, Thomas Hutchinson, asserting that a slave woman had written the book. The book was published in England with the help of Wheatley's patrons, the Countess of Huntington and the Earl of Dartmouth, after publishers in Boston refused.

PHILLIS WHEATLEY

WAS A SLAVE WHO WAS ORIGINALLY FROM WEST AFRICA. SHE BECAME THE FIRST AFRICAN AMERICAN TO PUBLISH A BOOK AND THE SECOND WOMAN IN THE UNITED STATES TO PUBLISH A COLLECTION OF POETRY. SHE IS CONSIDERED THE MOTHER OF THE AFRICAN-AMERICAN LITERARY TRADITION. HER WRITING ABILITIES SHOCKED WHITES OF HER DAY.

Wheatley is believed to have been brought from West Africa by a slave ship called the *Phillis*, which landed in Boston in 1761, when she was seven or eight. There, the wife of a wealthy local merchant bought her and taught her English and gave her a classical education. A child prodigy, Wheatley was observed trying to write letters on walls with chalk shortly after her arrival. She was fluent in English within 16 months of her arrival.

Wheatley, a frail young woman, published her first poem in 1770. On the advice of doctors, she sailed to England in 1773 with her mistress's son when her book was about to be published. She received a celebrity's welcome. In fact, Wheatley was so well received her owners were shamed into granting her freedom.

After her former mistress died in 1774, Wheatley tried to publish another volume of poetry, this time in America. She failed despite public praise.

Wheatley married a free Black man, John Peters, in 1778. During the political upheaval that followed Boston's fall to the British, Wheatley lived in poverty with her husband and three children. Two died. Wheatley died at age 31, in 1784, trying to support herself and her last remaining child.

Wheatley had her first poem published in 1770 in a Rhode Island newspaper, despite the fact that she arrived in America only six years earlier unable to speak English. In 1775, she wrote a poem honoring George Washington, prompting the commander in chief to invite her to visit.

WALTER F. WHITE

Thanks to Walter Francis White's outstanding organizational and administrative skills, the National Association for the Advancement of Colored People (NAACP) grew from a small group to the preeminent civil rights organization in America.

Under his leadership as secretary from 1931 to 1955, the NAACP greatly increased the number of its local branches, consolidated the dominance of African Americans within the body, and created the legal division that won so many key court battles that spurred the advancement of the Civil Rights Movement by ending legal segregation.

White's NAACP turned America's attention toward equal voting rights and the horrors of lynchings. It helped end all-White election primaries, restrictive housing practices, and legally sanctioned public discrimination.

It was under White's stewardship that the NAACP's legal division won the landmark *Brown* v. *Topeka, Kansas Board of Education* Supreme Court case in 1954, which outlawed segregation in public schools. The *Brown* case precipitated other court rulings that eventually ended all forms of public segregation and led to the enactment of civil rights legislation that championed equality of rights and opportunities for African Americans.

White was a blue-eyed, blonde-haired man who could have enjoyed a comfortable life passing for White. But he fought hard for racial justice because he was victimized several times in his life because he was African American. In fact, his father died of neglect in a Georgia hospital while doctors argued about whether or not he was Black.

White was born in Atlanta in 1893. At the age of 13, during an Atlanta race riot, White and his father sat inside with guns drawn as a mob threatened to invade their home. In 1916, after he graduated from Atlanta University, the city's school board was moving to limit public education for Blacks to sixth grade, while Whites could go on to high school. Atlanta's Black community formed an NAACP branch, with White as secretary, to combat the board, which eventually backed down on its plans.

White's actions caught the attention of James Weldon Johnson, then field secretary for the national organization. Johnson was influential in getting White a position in 1918 as assistant secretary.

Because of his complexion, White volunteered to investigate lynchings in the South since he could pass for White. He gained valuable information, even though he was almost lynched himself on one occasion. In 1920, White published his highly regarded *Rope and Faggot*, a major indictment of lynching in America.

In 1935 and again in 1940, as NAACP head, White lobbied to introduce federal anti-lynching legislation, which was defeated both times by proposed Senate filibusters. But those efforts turned national attention to the atrocities of lynching in the South and helped the NAACP become politically influential.

White organized the defense for innocent Blacks involved in the 1919 Chicago Race Riot. After Johnson became the NAACP's first Black

secretary in 1920, White worked with him for a decade. The organization flourished and White became invaluable as an administrator. He succeeded Johnson as secretary in 1931, the position he held until his death from a heart attack in 1955, when he was succeeded by his assistant Roy Wilkins.

Facing page: *White in his NAACP office in October 1948.* Above: *White (right) is joined by President Eisenhower (left) and Dr. Channing Tobias, chair of the NAACP, at the opening of the NAACP's Freedom Fulfillment Conference in 1954.*

DANIEL HALE WILLIAMS

Dr. Daniel Hale Williams was a pioneering surgeon who saved the life of a stabbing victim by performing the world's first heart surgery. He founded Provident Hospital in Chicago because other area hospitals refused an African-American woman a nursing education. Provident is the nation's oldest freestanding Black-owned hospital.

Williams created training programs for African-American nurses and interns, and was the only Black in the charter group of the American College of Surgeons. He also helped organize the National Medical Association, a professional organization for Black doctors.

Williams was born in Hollidaysburg, Pennsylvania, on January 18, 1856, one of seven children. At 17, Williams worked part-time in a barbershop while living with one of his sisters. He took a two-year apprenticeship with Dr. Henry Palmer, a legendary surgeon and former U.S. Surgeon General.

In the 1800s, many doctors began practicing after two years of training. But Williams went on to graduate from Chicago Medical College (later Northwestern Medical School) in 1883, opening his first office at 3034 South Michigan Avenue in Chicago. He was on the surgical staff at several institutions, taught anatomy, and in the late 1880s was appointed to the Illinois State Board of Health and was surgeon to the City Railway Company. Williams was the first Black to hold that position.

African-American doctors often performed surgery in people's homes at that time because hospitals refused to appoint Blacks to their staffs or to train Black nurses. So Williams pulled together a group of prestigious African-American and White doctors and founded Provident Hospital and Training School Association in 1891.

In 1893, on a hot July day, Williams saved the life of a stabbing victim by opening his chest and suturing a wound to the pericardium. The man lived for 20 years after the surgery. That same year, Williams was appointed Surgeon-in-Chief at Freedman's Hospital on the campus of Howard University in Washington, D.C.

In 1899, Williams was visiting professor at Meharry Medical College in Nashville. Returning to Chicago, Williams was on staff of Cook County Hospital from 1900 to 1906.

Ironically, leadership at Provident Hospital had passed to Dr. George Cleveland Hall, Williams's longtime antagonist. As a response to the increased segregation of Black life, the hospital board, under Hall's direction, required all physicians to bring all their patients

to the hospital. Because many of Williams's patients were White, board policy severed his relationship with the very hospital he founded.

In 1913, Williams became the first Black appointed as associate attending surgeon at St. Luke's Hospital in Chicago. He was also the only African American among the founders of the American College of Surgeons.

Williams suffered a series of strokes in the 1920s that ended his medical career, and he died on August 4, 1931.

Dr. Williams helped combat racism in the field of medicine by organizing the National Medical Association for African-American physicians, who, at the time, were not allowed to join the American Medical Association.

OPRAH WINFREY

Oprah Winfrey is an Emmy award-winning talk show host, an Academy-Award nominated actress, and one of the highest paid entertainers in America. She uses her position as the country's best-known talk show host to tackle issues affecting people's daily lives. *The Oprah Winfrey Show,* now handled by Winfrey's own production company, deals with social problems ranging from sexual abuse to racism and is watched by more than 17 million people daily. Winfrey is a testament to the resilience of the human spirit in the face of adversity and to the heights reachable through hard work. Her strength is her ability to make her guests and audience feel at home. Her emotional empathy for their problems is real.

The bubbly, voluble Winfrey had a stormy childhood. Born in a small Mississippi town to unmarried parents, Winfrey spent her early childhood with her grandmother. She was an exceptional child, making her first speaking appearance in church at the age of three. At age six, Winfrey moved to Milwaukee to live with her mother, Vernita Lee, but didn't fit into the subsistence-level existence Lee eked out on welfare and domestic work.

Winfrey lived briefly in Nashville, Tennessee, with her father, Vernon, but soon returned to her mother's home. The next few years were among the darkest in Winfrey's life. She was repeatedly sexually abused by a cousin and friends of the family. Vernon Winfrey brought his daughter back to Nashville, and she began to bloom under his strict guidance.

Despite her troubles, Winfrey was destined for great things. She was reporting the news for WVOL radio in Nashville before graduating from high school and continued in broadcasting as she started at Tennessee State University. Winfrey was the first woman television coanchor in town, at WTVF-TV. A few months before graduation, Winfrey moved to WJZ-TV in Baltimore, Maryland.

The talented Winfrey found her niche when the station made her cohost of its morning show, *People Are Talking.* Winfrey continued her meteoric rise in the field with a move to Chicago in 1984 to host WLS-TV's morning

show, *A.M. Chicago*, which became the top show in the market within three months. The show was renamed for Winfrey, went into syndication, and consistently gets phenomenal ratings. She has also expanded into film, with an Academy Award nomination for her first movie, *The Color Purple*.

As one of America's highest paid entertainers, Winfrey has contributed $1 million to Morehouse College, one of her many contributions to the community. She also uses her own company, Harpo Productions, to develop positive projects dealing with women and African Americans. Winfrey has received numerous awards, including the prestigious Peabody Award, both for her talk show and for her philanthropic work. She currently lives in Chicago along the lakefront.

Facing page: Winfrey enjoys working before the camera as much as she does producing entertainment events. She got a chance to do both when she produced and starred in the television miniseries The Women of Brewster Place. *Above: Winfrey taped a show on violence in the nation's schools at Southwestern High School in Baltimore.*

Carter G. Woodson arguably did more for the accurate study of Black Americans than any other historian. He opened the long neglected field of Black studies to scholars and also popularized the subject in Black schools and colleges.

Ironically, studying anything was something Woodson had to put off for quite a while. Born December 19, 1875, in New Canton, Virginia, he was the oldest of nine children of former slaves. Woodson could not attend school because his parents needed the money he earned in the coal mines.

Though unable to attend high school full-time until 1895, when he was 20 years old, the self-taught young man made up for lost time by graduating in less than two years. Admitted to Barea College in Kentucky, he earned his degree in 1903. Two years earlier, he had already earned a teaching certificate, which he used to teach in West Virginia high schools.

Through periodic semesterly visits and correspondence courses, Woodson received his bachelor's degree from the University of Chicago in 1908. Meanwhile, from 1903 to 1906,

he was a school supervisor in the Philippines and then spent 1906 and 1907 studying and traveling in Asia, North Africa, and Europe, including a semester at the University of Paris. In 1912, Woodson received his Ph.D. in history from Harvard University.

It's not clear why he had such an intense interest in the field of Black history—there were no courses in the subject offered during his collegiate work. Perhaps that was the reason. Still, in 1915, along with several other associates, Woodson formed the Association for the Study of Negro Life and History (ASNLH) in Chicago to encourage scholars to engage in the intensive study of the Black past.

Previously the field had been grossly maligned at the hands of White historians who accepted the traditionally biased perceptions of Black involvement in domestic and world affairs.

The ASNLH was primarily committed to historical research, training African-American historians, publishing texts about African-American life and history, collecting valuable or rare materials on the history of the race, and promoting that history through schools, churches, and fraternal groups.

From 1916 until his death in 1950, Woodson edited the *Journal of Negro History*, one of the premier historical publications in America during its time. From 1919 to 1920, Woodson was dean of the School of Liberal Arts and head of the graduate faculty at Howard University. From 1920 to 1922, he was dean at West Virginia State College. While there, Woodson founded Associated Publishers to produce accurate, scholarly books on Black life and culture.

In 1926, the stern and demanding academician founded Negro History Week to focus attention on Black contributions to civilization. The week was observed nationally and expanded into Black History Month in 1976 by proclamation of President Gerald Ford as part of the nation's bicentennial.

Woodson was writing a six-volume *Encyclopaedia Africana* at the time of his death. He died of a heart attack on April 3, 1950.

Woodson had a late start in education. He was self-taught until he was 20, when he finally attended high school. He then went on to study at the University of Chicago for his bachelor's degree and at Harvard University for his graduate work.

An important writer of the 20th century, Richard Wright was one of the first and most forceful authors to call attention to the consequences of racial exploitation of Blacks. His existential writings explored the recurring theme of how Black Americans live in a country whose structural racism denies their very humanity.

Wright's most compelling argument of this came in his 1940 novel *Native Son,* the raw and powerful story of Bigger Thomas, a young, Black man in Chicago who accidentally kills a White girl. Thomas then learns the depths of hostility that the White world harbors against Blacks.

Native Son was an international best-seller that quickly sold more than 300,000 copies; it was translated into six languages and it became a Book-of-the-Month Club selection.

Wright also turned the work into a powerful Broadway play, starring Canada Lee and staged by Orson Welles. In 1941, he won the Spingarn Award—the NAACP's highest book honor—for his novel. The book earned him fame and encouraged him to pursue a lifelong writing career.

Wright had come to the public's attention two years before with his *Uncle Tom's Children,* a collection of short stories released in 1938 that won the author a Guggenheim Fellowship. In these stories, Wright explored racial tensions in the rural South that most often ended in violence. With *Native Son,* he shifted locales to the big northern ghettos, where the same tensions culminated in the same results.

In 1945, Wright published his autobiography, *Black Boy,* which has become an American classic. Also selected as a Book-of-the-Month Club selection, *Black Boy* was translated into six languages and outsold *Native Son.* The story is about Wright's early childhood in the South through his young adulthood in Chicago. The book examines the painful workings of the racist social order.

Wright was born near Natchez, Mississippi, on September 4, 1908, and grew up in poverty in orphanages and with various family mem-

---

RICHARD WRIGHT WAS ONE OF THE FIRST WRITERS OF PROTEST FICTION DECRYING WHITE MISTREATMENT OF BLACKS IN AMERICA. HIS MOST NOTED WORK IS THE NOVEL NATIVE SON, *WHICH DETAILED THE LIFE AND DEATH OF BIGGER THOMAS, A CHICAGO BLACK MAN WHO ACCIDENTALLY KILLS A WHITE GIRL. THE 1940 BEST-SELLER WON WRIGHT THE NAACP'S SPINGARN MEDAL.*

Facing page: *Wright in his Paris living room, in 1949. The author left America to live in France in the mid-1940s after growing increasingly disillusioned with American racism.* Left: *Wright's later writing efforts included* The Outsider, *which he completed in 1953. The novel is considered by many to be among the first existential works.*

bers. It was a dismal childhood that gave him a dark outlook on life.

He had trouble adjusting to southern racism and Jim Crow segregation. He determined that if he was to survive, he had to go North to live. Wright moved to Memphis in 1925 and two years later he moved to Chicago, where he worked odd jobs until being ac-

cepted into the Federal Writers Project during the Depression.

After the success of *Black Boy,* Wright, disturbed by American racism and having found more freedom in his travels abroad, left America. He lived the rest of his life in Paris, where he died of a heart attack November 28, 1960, at the age of 52.

MALCOLM X

AS THE PRIMARY SPOKESMAN FOR THE NATION OF ISLAM FOR A DOZEN YEARS, MALCOLM X CAPTIVATED THE COUNTRY WITH HIS PASSIONATE SPEECH ABOUT THE ANGER AND FRUSTRATION FELT BY BLACKS BECAUSE OF THE DEVASTATING EFFECTS OF RACISM. HE FORCEFULLY CHALLENGED WHITE DOMINION, DEMANDED CHANGE, AND HELPED INSPIRE RACIAL PRIDE IN MANY AFRICAN AMERICANS.

Perhaps no one else in the Civil Rights Movement gave as forceful a voice to the rage and frustration of Black Americans as Malcolm X. As he passionately spoke to America, Malcolm brazenly challenged White domination and demanded change. In so doing, he struck a nerve with a large segment of the Black population, many of whom began to find self-respect and racial pride.

Malcolm's style and message stood in stark contrast to his leadership peers in the Movement, who favored nonviolent protests and integration to end discrimination. Malcolm believed in fighting back if attacked, calling it unmanly not to do so. He also felt that integration was demeaning; that it would lead to only token accommodation by Whites. He believed that it would have no effect on the urban Black underclass.

Malcolm was a nationalist who believed in Black self-reliance—that African Americans should control their own institutions, economy, and politics. He preached that this self-determination would have to be realized "by any means necessary."

He rose to prominence as the national spokesman for the Nation of Islam, a Black separatist group (also known as the Black Muslims) under the leadership of Elijah Muhammad. The Muslims taught that Blacks were the original human race with an impressive culture and civilization until they were enslaved by Whites. Black Muslims taught that only by returning to their true religion, Islam, could Black Americans recapture their rightful heritage.

As the Nation of Islam's representative for a dozen years (1952–1964), Malcolm was a brilliant, powerful orator who attracted huge crowds on the university lecture circuit and had a constant media following. He increased Muslim membership by traveling the country and telling African Americans about their previous rich culture, which he said had been taken away by Whites who had then brainwashed Blacks into a mentality of self-hate. Malcolm pointed to the Muslims and Islam as the way to a better life, using his own life as an example. He proved it was possible to readjust one's life path.

He was born on May 19, 1925, in Omaha, Nebraska, as Malcolm Little. His family was forced out of Omaha by White vigilantes who burned down the family's house. The Littles resettled in Lansing, Michigan, where, in 1931, Malcolm's Baptist minister father was killed, supposedly by Whites. After his mother was institutionalized from the strain of trying to raise her family, the children were separated and sent to various foster homes.

Malcolm went to Boston to live with a relative, but fell into a life of crime—selling and using drugs, running numbers, and organizing a burglary ring. These activities landed him in jail at the age of 21 for six years.

While imprisoned, he was introduced to the teachings of Elijah Muhammad; those teachings allowed him to vent his anger at the way Whites had treated his family and denied him opportunities.

Malcolm began to accept Muslim ideology, which stresses fastidiousness of mind and

Left: *In 1964, Malcolm wanted Black leaders to form a civil rights organization to bring the plight of African Americans before the United Nations.* Right: *Malcolm meets with Martin Luther King, Jr., whom he frequently ridiculed for his nonviolent tactics. But before he died, Malcolm tried to make amends with King.*

Below: Malcolm addresses a Harlem rally in June 1963. Later in the year, he called the assassination of President John Kennedy a "case of chickens coming home to roost"—an example of the kind of violence Whites in America had long used against Blacks. Facing page: Malcolm leaves his house the day after it was firebombed in February 1965. He and his family were uninjured by the Molotov cocktails that exploded in his living room during the night. However, Malcolm was assassinated the next week while delivering a speech in New York City.

body and allows no unclean habits. He improved his intellect by copying every word of the dictionary and reading voraciously.

After his parole in 1952, Malcolm intensified his Muslim studies and dropped the last name Little and took X, the Muslim designation for an African American's original lost African surname. In 1954, Muhammad, whom Malcolm at first worshiped, made him a minister. Through the years, Malcolm headed Muslim mosques in Boston, Philadelphia, and Harlem and organized dozens of temples around the country. He also founded *Muhammad Speaks,* a newspaper that would later denounce him.

But Malcolm's growing popularity became a source of contention within the Nation, and his discovery of Muhammad's alleged immoral personal behavior created a schism. Malcolm left the Muslims in 1964.

He organized two groups of his own, the Muslim Mosque Inc. and the Organization of African-American Unity. To undergird his religious beliefs in opening his own mosque, Malcolm took a pilgrimage to the Islamic holy land of Mecca, Saudi Arabia.

Malcolm encountered worshipers of all colors who embraced him in brotherhood. This made him reconsider his indictment of all White-skinned people as being evil "devils," and he revised his separatist notions. After this pilgrimage, he changed his name to El-Hajj Malik El-Shabazz.

Upon his conversion to orthodox Islam and his return to America, Malcolm denounced Muhammad, which lead to an increasingly bitter and open feud. He expanded his interests in civil rights to include human rights worldwide and even sought to make partial amends with leaders of the Civil Rights Movement, especially Dr. Martin Luther King, Jr.

But on February 21, 1965, just one week after his house had been firebombed, Malcolm X was assassinated.

WHITNEY M. YOUNG, JR.

Whitney M. Young, Jr., was a calming voice in the midst of the militant Civil Rights Movement of the 1960s. As executive director of the National Urban League, Young worked to keep communication open with White America's centers of financial and political power. He did so in order to give concrete help to African Americans. Critics feared Young had too many close ties to Whites. Yet he brought millions of dollars to the Urban League, increased the number of branches, and gathered government support that might have been lacking.

Young was born in Lincoln Ridge, Kentucky, on July 21, 1921. After getting his bachelor's degree at Kentucky State College in 1941, he taught briefly before joining the U.S. Army during World War II. Young then studied electrical engineering at the Massachusetts Institute of Technology. His experiences with racism in the military turned Young toward the civil rights struggle.

Young received his master's degree from the University of Minnesota and started working with the Urban League. He worked at branch offices in two states at a time when the organization was focused more on housing and health issues than with civil rights. In 1954, Young became dean of the Atlanta University School of Social Work. The articulate, personable Young spent a year at Harvard University under a Rockefeller Foundation grant in 1960, then began a brilliant career as executive director of the National Urban League.

Before Young's involvement, the group was training Black social workers to fight for improvements in housing, sanitation, and other self-improvement issues. It left the civil rights fight to more militant African-American organizations. Young leaped with both feet into the fray. He dealt with social problems by influencing White decision makers and becoming part of the process for change.

Critics called Young an "Uncle Tom," but he increased the Urban League's budget from $250,000 and 34 staff in 1961 to $3,500,000 and 200 staff by 1968. He created jobs and opened 90 new regional branches. Young, fighting to

Facing page: *Young frequently had the ear of President Lyndon Johnson, with whom he would discuss racial issues in America.* Left: *In December 1963, shortly after Johnson assumed the presidency, Young petitioned him to undertake a "crash effort" to ease unemployment among Blacks, including establishing a public works program.*

keep his credibility among Blacks, proposed a national Marshall plan in 1963 to help African Americans catch up. His book, *To Be Equal,* documents his vision. One quote from his book is an example of that vision, "Good race relations—race harmony—is more than the absence of conflict, tension, or even war. *It is the presence of justice.* Nothing is more immoral than the suggestion that people adjust to injustice or that we make a god of 'timing.' The time is always ripe to do right."

During the sixties, American leaders turned to Young and leaders such as Dr. Martin Luther King, Jr., to calm the voices of more militant Black leaders. Young stayed at the front of the struggle, helping to organize the 1963 March on Washington, D.C. Young published *Beyond Racism: Building an Open Society* in 1969, which explained that the Black power era could help the nation move toward a more democratic society.

Young's brilliant career was cut short when he drowned in 1971 in Africa, while attending a conference.

INDEX